DEVELOPMENTAL NEUROPSYCHOLOGY, *18*(1), 1–10

A Life-Span Perspective on Interaction Between the Cerebral Hemispheres

Marie T. Banich
The Beckman Institute
Department of Psychology
University of Illinois at Urbana–Champaign

Warren S. Brown
Travis Research Institute,
Fuller Graduate School of Psychology
Department of Psychiatry and Biobehavioral Sciences,
University of California at Los Angeles

This issue of *Developmental Neuropsychology* is designed to examine recent advances in our understanding of how interaction between the cerebral hemispheres can change with age. An enhanced appreciation of the degree to which lateralization of function influences mental processing was spurred by research in the 1970s and beyond (e.g., Davidson & Hugdahl, 1995). The knowledge that the left hemisphere is best suited for processing information in a piecemeal, analytic manner, whereas the right hemisphere is best suited for processing information in a holistic or gestalt manner has filtered down to popular culture, as reflected in everything from advertisements to songs. Such representations often depict the hemispheres as unlikely bedfellows—the verbal left hemisphere and the spatial right hemisphere, or the analytic left hemisphere and the intuitive right hemisphere. Research with split-brain patients was startling, because in the absence of a corpus callosum, which normally functions to integrate the activity of the hemispheres, each hemisphere's abilities appeared in stark relief. By disconnecting them, it became clear exactly what an "odd couple" the hemispheres are.

Given that lateralization of function is a hallmark of human brain organization, it seems increasingly important to investigate how such seemingly ill-suited part-

Requests for reprints should be sent to Marie T. Banich, Department of Psychology, University of Colorado at Boulder, UCB 345, Boulder, CO 80309. E-mail: mbanich@psych.colorado.edu

ners ever manage to integrate their processing to produce the seamless behavior that we all experience. Of course, this question of the consequences of functional connectivity between brain regions is not limited to questions of how the hemispheres interact (e.g., Paus et al., 1997). However, using interaction between the hemispheres to address this fundamental question of brain organization is particularly attractive for a number of reasons. First, investigating hemispheric integration is experimentally very tractable in a noninvasive manner. Furthermore, knowledge gained from studies of intact individuals can be examined against the backdrop of the large body of research that has examined individuals who have had the cerebral commissures surgically severed (split-brain patients); individuals in whom the corpus callosum has failed to develop (i.e., those with agenesis of the corpus callosum [ACC]); and those with suspected damage to callosal fibers caused by disease or trauma (phenylketonuria, multiple sclerosis, traumatic brain injury).

The articles in this issue investigate some of the important questions regarding integration of information between the hemispheres from a life-span perspective, ranging from childhood through the older adult years. These articles include information from individuals of differing age with intact commissures, those with congenital absence of the corpus callosum, and those with presumed disease-related callosal damage—allowing for the strength of converging perspectives.

THE CORPUS CALLOSUM AND CHILD DEVELOPMENT

From a developmental perspective, one of the most important structural changes in the brain that is likely to affect interhemispheric interaction is the increasing myelination of the corpus callosum. Although the classic work on callosal development (Yakovlev & Lecours, 1967), which was based on postmortem samples, suggested that this process was completed by late childhood, the advent of magnetic resonance imaging has revealed that myelination continues much later than was initially thought. Increases in callosal myelination occur well into the late teenage years, suggesting that the corpus callosum is one of the latest structures to myelinate (Giedd et al., 1996). Hence, a primary question of interest is whether these changes in myelination have behavioral consequences. This question is addressed in a variety of ways in different articles within this issue.

Hagelthorn, Brown, Amano, and Asarnow (this issue) examined two measures of interhemispheric processing—one physiological and the other behavioral—and determined their relation. Because advancing age during childhood is associated with increased myelination and decreased interhemispheric transfer time, it has been assumed that decreased transfer time would have behavioral consequences. Hagelthorn et al. put this idea to the test. They obtained estimates of interhemispheric transfer time from visual event-related potentials (ERPs) acquired during performance of a matching task. This task examined the degree to which match decisions were facilitated when two items to be compared were divided across the hemispheres rather than being directed to the same hemisphere (i.e., the degree of the bilateral field advantage). These researchers found clear evidence of a reduced bilateral field advantage with age and a trend indicating a reduction in interhemispheric transfer time based on the N1 (first negative wave) component of the ERP. However, the two measures were not significantly correlated, indicating that they may measure different aspects of callosal function. Nevertheless, these data provide evidence that age-related increases in myelination have a behavioral consequence in more rapid interhemispheric transfer and more accurate and efficient comparison of the information between the hemispheres.

Corroborating this viewpoint is another article within this issue. Chicoine, Proteau, and Lassonde (this issue) found that the incomplete callosal myelination in young children can have rather severe behavioral consequences. They demonstrate that the corpus callosum of young children aged 6 to 7 years cannot support the transfer of a learned visuomotor skill from one hand (and hence one hemisphere) to the other. In a particularly elegant demonstration, these authors show the striking similarity between the performances of young children and those of individuals with ACC who lack a corpus callosum, revealing how inadequate the immature callosum is for transferring certain types of information.

In contrast, the article by Banich, Passarotti, and Janes (this issue) suggests a developmental trend in bilateral visual matching that is somewhat different than that reported by Hagelthorn et al. (this issue) and that appears to be the consequence of intrahemispheric limitations in processing resources. In adults, interaction between the hemispheres is more beneficial to performance when tasks are computationally complex as compared to simple (e.g., Banich & Belger, 1990; Belger & Banich, 1992). This division of processing, allowed by a hemispheric splitting and then callosal reintegration of information, also appears to be especially helpful whenever the computational resources of particular individuals are taxed. For the most complex version of the Banich, Passarotti, and Janes task, younger school-age children showed evidence of benefitting more from a division of processing than did older children; that is, they showed a larger bilateral advantage.

It is instructive to consider both the convergence and divergence among these studies. Even though they use children of different age ranges and different methods, there is a convergence in that these studies all suggest that interhemispheric interaction changes during childhood. The studies diverge in that they suggest different developmental changes for different tasks or measures of interhemispheric interaction and callosal function. In many ways, divergent findings are not surprising. First, there are differences across the studies in task and stimulus complexity, as already mentioned. Although both Hagelthorn et al. (this issue) and Banich, Passarotti, and Janes (this issue) used bilateral and unilateral letter-matching tasks, the complexities of the tasks were very different, and the consequent outcomes with respect to child development differed. The bilateral advantage that was larger in older children who performed the very simple matching task of Hagelthorn et al. became a bilateral advantage that was larger with younger children who performed the much more computationally complex task of Banich, Passarotti, and Janes. Apparently the simpler task could be done well by a single hemisphere. Thus, an increasing bilateral advantage with age reflected the ease of callosal transfer. However, the Banich, Passarotti, and Janes task exhausted the information-processing resources of the single hemisphere of the younger child; thus, an additional variable came into play—that of the computational gain provided by dividing processing across the hemispheres. In the study of Chicoine et al. (this issue), bihemispheric stimulus comparisons were not at issue. Nevertheless, the complex motor skill that was learned by the dominant hand (hemisphere) did not transfer to the other hemisphere in the younger children, whereas transfer was clearly present for older children. Here the critical variable is the insufficient channel capacity of the corpus callosum to mediate transfer of a complex learned motor skill.

In addition, divergent findings may relate to the fact that different tasks place demands on different callosal channels. The corpus callosum consists of over 250 million nerve fibers, and different sections of the callosum are likely to be tapped by the different paradigms used in these studies. For example, the measures of interhemispheric transfer time derived from the visual ERP likely reflect functioning of the splenium of the corpus callosum, which interconnects regions of extrastriate cortex, which is the where the visual N1 is generated (Brown, Jeeves, Dietrich, & Burnison, 1999; Clark & Hillyard, 1996; Simpson, Foxe, Vaughan, Mehta, & Schroeder, 1995). In contrast, the visuomotor learning task used by Chicoine et al. (this issue) is more likely to reflect functioning of parietal or central cortices, and hence of regions of the callosum more anterior to the splenium. It is not clear exactly what portion of the callosum is required by the Banich and Belger task used by Banich, Passarotti, and Janes (this issue) or by the matching task used by Hagelthorn et al. (this issue), although results from a patient with anterior section of the callosum (Copeland & Zaidel, 1997) indicate that such regions may be critical in both tasks. Finally, it appears that interhemispheric interactions can be asymmetric even within the same callosal pathways (Brown, Larson, & Jeeves, 1994). This asymmetry may be subject to a developmental process. These results suggest that although we talk about *interhemispheric interaction,* that term probably really reflects a family of means and mechanisms of interchange that may more appropriately be termed *interhemispheric interactions.*

LIFE-SPAN CHANGES IN INTERHEMISPHERIC INTERACTIONS

Other articles in this issue consider life-span topics from the perspective of both young children and aged adults. Using the dichotic listening task as a proxy for interhemispheric interaction, Cowell and Hugdahl (this issue) examined the various aspects of individual differences that may influence this function. In particular, they examined effects of gender and handedness, which have been discussed for over a decade as having an effect on callosal morphology (e.g., Witelson & Goldsmith, 1991). Their results indicate that the effects of these variables are likely to be interactive, which suggests that uncovering the exact nature of the relations of these characteristics to callosal function in dichotic listening is likely to be somewhat daunting.

In addition to effects of gender and handedness on callosal functioning, there is also evidence of the effects of adult aging. The article by Reuter-Lorenz and Stanczak (this issue) shows that with age there is a greater benefit from interhemispheric interaction at lower levels of computational complexity. This finding suggests a greater need for division of information processing between the hemispheres with advancing age, which the authors link very nicely to functional neuroimaging studies of aging. One pattern found in neuroimaging studies of aged individuals is that the elderly are more likely to show bilateral activation, as compared with younger adults (e.g., Cabeza et al., 1997). Rather than positing a breakdown of localization of function, known as *dedifferentiation,* Reuter-Lorenz and Stanczak proposed on the basis of the interhemispheric work that this pattern of bilateral activation in the aged brain reflects an invoking of mechanism of interhemispheric interaction to deal with the reduced computational capacity of the single hemisphere.

INTERHEMISPHERIC INTERACTIONS AND COMPROMISED CALLOSAL INTEGRITY

Another theme of the articles within this issue is how we can be informed about interaction between the hemispheres by examining interchange in individuals who lack or have compromised callosal function. The article by Chicoine et al. (this issue) provides a striking display of how the performance of young children, aged 6 to 7 years, on a visuomotor task looks very similar to the performance of individuals who lack a callosum and have only an anterior commissure available for direct cortical–cortical transfer. The converging perspective provided by such evidence allows us to have much greater certainty that the deficit observed in young children on the same task is the consequence of immature callosal function, rather than limitations in intrahemispheric processing resources.

The article by Banich, Passarotti, White, Nortz, and Steiner (this issue) takes a different perspective in examining a population of children, those with early-treated phenylketonuria (ETPKU), who are likely to have atypical myelination, which would affect the corpus callosum. Unlike neurologically intact young children, who seem to rely on an even greater degree of interaction between the hemispheres to compensate for computational complexity, children with ETPKU do not appear to have such an option available to them. Apparently, reduced callosal function due to the phenylketonuria reduces callosal interactions such that interhemispheric sharing of information is diminished. As a result, bihemispheric sharing of processing is not advantageous, and children with ETPKU do not exhibit the typical across-hemisphere advantage.

A SUMMARY OF THE DYNAMICS OF INTERHEMISPHERIC INTERACTIONS AND CALLOSAL FUNCTION

Given all these different perspectives that are provided by life-span studies, can we come to some general conclusions about callosal function? We believe that there are some common themes that are revealed across this series of articles. Expanding somewhat on the Banich and Belger (1990) model, we would theorize that there are three major factors that influence callosal interactions and that determine whether dividing processing across the hemispheres is helpful to task performance. These factors are (a) the degree to which the processing resources of a single hemisphere are taxed by the computational complexity of the task in a given individual, (b) the degree to which a communication overhead is imposed by callosal transfer, and (c) whether the informational complexity of the stimulus to be transferred exceeds the channel capacity of the callosum (or of the noncallosal commissures) of the individual.

The work presented within this issue provides support for such a conceptualization. The work of Banich and colleagues (Banich & Belger, 1990; Belger & Banich, 1992, 1998) has demonstrated that when tasks are computationally simple, it is actually advantageous to have information be processed by a single hemisphere. Because the processing resources of one hemisphere are ample for the task, only the communication overhead imposed by callosal transfer slows processing. On such tasks, bilateral disadvantages are seen, and the degree of disadvantage suggests the functional state of the callosum.

A similar issue is the complexity of the stimulus material itself, particularly with respect to the channel capacity of the corpus callosum, anterior commissure, and other pathways available. Here, the prediction is that individuals without a corpus callosum should not exhibit much of a transfer deficit for very simple stimuli, and this is indeed the case (Kreuter, Kinsbourne, & Trevarthen, 1972). In fact, there are some simple across-hemisphere matching tasks that can be done in the absence of the corpus callosum. What these studies reveal, however, is that the complexity of the information influences whether it can be transferred by noncallosal fibers. Work by Brown et al. (1999) reveals that ACC individuals with only an anterior commissure can transfer information about simple, overlearned, and easily encoded stimuli (such as letters), especially when the set of possible items and responses is limited. However, as the information complexity of the stimuli to be transferred increases (e.g., complex visual patterns that cannot easily be labeled), the available anterior commissure cannot support transfer. Jeeves and Lamb (1988) made a similar argument regarding callosal channel capacity in a study in which the information necessary for interhemispheric stimulus comparisons could be measured in bits.

When task complexity increases to the point that the resources of a single hemisphere are overly taxed, another process comes into play. Under such conditions, it becomes advantageous to divide processing across the hemispheres so that more computational power can be brought to bear. Because both hemispheres can process almost all tasks to some degree (and perhaps in different manners), division of processing is possible. In such a case, it is assumed that the extra computational power brought to bear by interhemispheric division of processing more than offsets the overhead involved in callosal communication.

Let us examine the way in which such a model can explain the findings from the different clinical populations examined in this issue. In the elderly adults, we assume that each hemisphere has less computational power than that possessed by corresponding hemispheres of younger adults. Under such a conceptualization, the ability of a given hemisphere is more likely to be taxed at a lower level of complexity than in young adults, and there is a consequent need to switch to an across-hemisphere processing mode at a lower stage of computational complexity. Such a possibility is supported by recent data that demonstrated that the brain appears to be able to switch flexibly between a within- and an across-hemisphere mode of processing (or vice versa), depending on task demands (Weissman & Banich, 2000). Although there may be some loss of callosal connections in older adults (Janowsky, Kaye, & Carper, 1996), these probably do not yield an exaggerated effect of aging as compared to the effects of aging on the processing capacity of the cerebral cortex itself. Thus, because intrahemispheric resources are exceeded more readily in older adults, relatively more intact callosal function allows for greater advantages to accrue from splitting processing demands between the hemispheres. Hence, the greater bilateral advantage demonstrated at lower levels of task complexity in the aged probably reflects loss of intrahemispheric processing resources.

The inability of younger children to perform the visuomotor task used by Chicoine et al. (this issue) when tested with the unpracticed hand appears to be due not to limitations in intrahemispheric resources, but rather to the complexity of the information that must be transferred interhemispherically. The finding that individuals with ACC also fail to transfer the learning to the unpracticed hand suggests that the information that must be transferred is too complex for alternative interhemispheric pathways. Hence, the lack of across-hemisphere transfer in younger children in this task probably reflects limitations in the channel capacity of the corpus callosum. Brown and Paul (2000) made similar comparisons between child development and callosal agenesis with respect to reduced interhand transfer of the complex tactile–spatial information of the Tactile Performance Test.

Finally, with regard to children with ETPKU, there is no evidence that they exhibit a deficit on within-hemisphere trials compared with their neurologically intact peers. This suggests that the computational complexity of each hemisphere is not being disproportionately taxed in ETPKU as compared with age-matched individuals. Rather, either the lack of callosal myelination increases the general overhead of callosal transfer (i.e., increases interhemispheric transfer time) or, as in younger children, the callosum has been adversely affected so that it cannot support transfer of more complex information (i.e., channel capacity has been exceeded).

SOME REMAINING RESEARCH QUESTIONS

Although such a framework may help to explain some aspects of callosal function, there is another class of questions, not addressed by articles in this issue, that will need to be addressed in future work for us to adequately understand the nature of interhemispheric interaction. In the articles included in this issue, most of the authors have centered their investigations on how the corpus callosum affects the information-processing capacity of the brain across the life span. They do not address the question of the nature of the representation of information that is transferred across the hemispheres. For example, they do not answer the question of how facial features analyzed by the left hemisphere are integrated with information about the gestalt of a face processed by the right hemisphere. How do these two types of information get integrated? Stated metaphorically, if the left hemisphere is thinking in French and the right in English, what language do they use to communicate—French? English? or some other language? Does the "language" of interhemispheric interactions and callosal transfer change with age, with changes in callosal integrity, or with different task demands? We hope that this issue serves to provoke a larger discussion about how information processing is integrated across the hemispheres (and between other brain regions) over the process of life-span development.

REFERENCES

Banich, M. T., & Belger, A. (1990). Interhemispheric interaction: How do the hemispheres divide and conquer a task? *Cortex, 26,* 77–94.

Banich, M. T., Passarotti, A. M., & Janes, D. (2000/this issue). Interhemispheric interaction during childhood: I. Neurologically intact children. *Developmental Neuropsychology, 18,* 33–51.

Banich, M. T., Passarotti, A. M., White, D. A., Nortz, M. J., & Steiner, R. D. (2000/this issue). Interhemispheric interaction during childhood: II. Children with early-treated phenylketonuria. *Developmental Neuropsychology, 18,* 53–71.

Belger, A., & Banich, M. T. (1992). Interhemispheric interaction affected by computational complexity. *Neuropsychologia, 30,* 923–931.

Belger, A., & Banich, M. T. (1998). Costs and benefits of integrating information between the cerebral hemispheres: A computational perspective. *Neuropsychology, 12,* 380–398.

Brown, W. S., Jeeves, M. A., Dietrich, R., & Burnison, D. S. (1999). Bilateral field advantage and evoked potential interhemispheric transmission in commissurotomy and callosal agenesis. *Neuropsychologia, 37,* 1165–1180.

Brown, W. S., Larson, E. B., & Jeeves, M. A. (1994). Directional asymmetries in interhemispheric transfer time: Evidence from visual evoked potentials. *Neuropsychologia, 32,* 439–448.

Brown, W. S., & Paul, L. K. (2000). Cognitive and psychosocial deficits in agenesis of the corpus callosum with normal intelligence. *Cognitive Neuropsychiatry, 5,* 135–157.

Cabeza, R., Grady, C. L., Nyberg, L., McIntosh, A. R., Tulving, E., Kapur, S., Jennings, J. M., Houle, S., & Craik, F. I. M. (1997). Age-related differences in neural activity during memory encoding and retrieval: A positron emission tomography study. *Journal of Neuroscience, 17,* 391–400.

Chicoine, A.-J., Proteau, L., & Lassonde, M. (2000/this issue). Absence of interhemispheric transfer of unilateral visuomotor learning in young children and individuals with agenesis of the corpus callosum. *Developmental Neuropsychology, 18,* 73–94.

Clark, V. P., & Hillyard, S. A. (1996). Spatial selective attention affects early extrastriate but not striate components of the visual evoked potential. *Journal of Cognitive Neuroscience, 8,* 387–402.

Copeland, S. A., & Zaidel, E. (1997). Callosal channels and the bilateral distribution advantage: Patterns in agenesis and partial section of the corpus callosum [Abstract]. *Journal of the International Neuropsychological Society, 3,* 50.

Cowell, P., & Hugdahl, K. (2000/this issue). Individual differences in neurobehavioral measures of laterality and interhemispheric function as measured by dichotic listening. *Developmental Neuropsychology, 18,* 95–112.

Davidson, R. J., & Hugdahl, K. (Eds.). (1995). *Brain asymmetry.* Cambridge, MA: MIT Press.

Giedd, J. N., Rumsey, J. M., Castellanos, F. X., Rajapakse, J. C., Kaysen, D., Vaituzis, A. C., Vauss, Y. C., Hamburger, S. D., & Rapoport, J. L. (1996). A quantitative MRI study of the corpus callosum in children and adolescents. *Brain Research: Developmental Brain Research, 91,* 274–280.

Hagelthorn, K. M., Brown, W. S., Amano, S., & Asarnow, R. (2000/this issue). Normal development of bilateral field advantage and evoked potential interhemispheric transmission time. *Developmental Neuropsychology, 18,* 11–31.

Janowsky, J. S., Kaye, J. A., & Carper, R. A. (1996). Atrophy of the corpus callosum in Alzheimer's disease versus healthy aging. *Journal of the American Geriatrics Society, 44,* 798–803.

Jeeves, M. A., & Lamb, A. (1988). Cerebral asymmetries and interhemispheric processes. *Behavioural Brain Research, 29,* 211–223.

Kreuter, C., Kinsbourne, M., & Trevarthen, C. (1972). Are deconnected cerebral hemispheres independent channels? *Neuropsychologia, 10,* 453–461.

Paus, T., Jech, R., Thompson, C. J., Comeau, R., Peters, T., & Evans, A. C. (1997). Transcranial magnetic stimulation during positron emission tomography—A new method for studying connectivity of the human cerebral cortex. *Journal of Neuroscience, 17,* 3178–3184.

Reuter-Lorenz, P. A., & Stanczak, L. (2000/this issue). Differential effects of aging on the functions of the corpus callosum. *Developmental Neuropsychology, 18,* 113–137.

Simpson, G. V., Foxe, J. J., Vaughan, J. G., Mehta, A. D., & Schroeder, C. E. (1995). Integration of electrophysiological source analyses, MRI and animal models in the study of visual processing and attention. *Electroencephalography and Clinical Neurophysiology,* (Suppl. 44), 76–92.

Weissman, D. H., & Banich, M. T. (2000). The cerebral hemispheres cooperate to perform complex but not simple tasks. *Neuropsychology, 14,* 41–59.

Witelson, S. F., & Goldsmith, C. H. (1991). The relationship of hand preference to anatomy of the corpus callosum in men. *Brain Research, 545,* 175–182.

Yakovlev, P. I., & Lecours, A. R. (1967). The myelogenetic cycles of regional maturation of the brain. In A. Minkowski (Ed.), *Regional development of the brain in early life* (pp. 3–70). Oxford, England: Blackwell.

DEVELOPMENTAL NEUROPSYCHOLOGY, *18*(1), 11–31

Normal Development of Bilateral Field Advantage and Evoked Potential Interhemispheric Transmission Time

Kathleen M. Hagelthorn
Kennedy Krieger Institute
Johns Hopkins University School of Medicine

Warren S. Brown
Travis Research Institute,
Fuller Graduate School of Psychology
Department of Psychiatry and Biobehavioral Sciences,
University of California at Los Angeles

Stacy Amano
Travis Research Institute
Fuller Graduate School of Psychology

Robert Asarnow
Department of Psychiatry and Biobehavioral Sciences
University of California at Los Angeles

Implications of the developmental progression of myelination of the corpus callosum were studied using evoked potential interhemispheric transmission time (EP-IHTT) and the bilateral field advantage (BFA) in letter matching. Forty-two normal children aged 7 to 17 years were asked to respond regarding whether 2 letters matched when presented either unilaterally (both in the same visual field) or bilaterally (1 letter in each field). Evoked potentials were recorded with bilateral midparietal electrodes during unilateral presentations of the letter-matching task. Age-related changes were found for both EP-IHTT and BFA. BFA in reaction time in the visual letter-matching

Requests for reprints should be sent to Warren S. Brown, Travis Research Institute, 180 N. Oakland Avenue, Pasadena, CA 91101. E-mail: wsbrown@fuller.edu

task increased significantly with age. Decreasing EP-IHTT with age was also evident (although only in a statistical trend). These findings lend support to the hypothesis that increased callosal myelination during late childhood has functional significance. Callosal maturation appears to result in faster interhemispheric transfer and increasing ability to integrate information across the midline.

Neuroanatomical research suggests that myelination of the long intracortical connective pathways is an important part of childhood brain development. Among the last pathways to develop is the corpus callosum, which does not become fully myelinated until sometime during the second decade of life (Giedd et al., 1996; Yakovlev & Lecours, 1967). Atypical communication between the hemispheres due to developmental abnormalities of the corpus callosum has been proposed as a possible contributor to a variety of neuropsychological disorders including dyslexia (Hynd, Semrud-Clikeman, Lorys, Novey, & Eliopulos, 1990; Markee, Brown, Moore, & Theberge, 1996; Moore, Brown, Markee, Theberge, & Zvi, 1995, 1996), attention deficit hyperactivity disorder (Hynd et al., 1991), learning disabilities (Njiokiktjien, de Sonneville, & Vaal, 1994), mental retardation (Bodensteiner, Schaefer, Breeding, & Cowan, 1994), autism (Belmonte, Egaas, Townsend, & Courchesne, 1995), Tourette syndrome (Baumgardner et al., 1996), and schizophrenia (David, 1993; Raine et al., 1990). Given the late development of the corpus callosum and its potential role in neurocognitive abilities, this research was undertaken to investigate the neurophysiological and perceptual correlates of the progressive development of the corpus callosum in normal children.

NEUROANATOMICAL DEVELOPMENT OF THE CORPUS CALLOSUM

Data from postmortem and imaging studies suggest that myelination of the corpus callosum is an ongoing process during childhood that continues through at least the early teenage years, if not later. Yakovlev and Lecours (1967) studied the myelination of the corpus callosum by staining and measuring myelinated fibers from the brains of over 200 normal infants from the fourth fetal month through the first postnatal year and brains from individuals in the third and fourth decades of life, as well as the brains of a few in the first and second decades of life. They found that the corpus callosum begins to myelinate around the fourth postnatal month and continues until approximately age 10, with some evidence of continued myelination even after that point.

Recent research has used magnetic resonance imaging (MRI) to measure changes in development in the size and morphology of the corpus callosum (Barkovich & Maroldo, 1993; Giedd et al., 1996; Ono et al., 1993; Pujol, Vendrell, Junqué, Martì-Vilalta, & Capdevila, 1993; Rajapakse et al., 1996). Giedd et al.

(1996; Rajapakse et al., 1996) found that midsagittal callosal size increased linearly between 4 and 18 years in both male and female normal children. Pujol et al. (1993) assessed the rate of growth of the corpus callosum by obtaining two MRIs, taken approximately 2 years apart, on 90 participants. They found evidence of continued growth of the corpus callosum up to the middle 20s. They concluded that the corpus callosum continues to mature at a rate that parallels continued human behavioral maturation.

Increases in callosal size during child development may have either of two possible sources. One possibility is that larger size suggests more complete myelination, as suggested in the work of Yakovlev and Lecours (1967). Another interpretation is provided by the work of Aboitiz (1992; Aboitiz, Scheibel, Fisher, & Zaidel, 1992), who demonstrated that between-subject difference in size reflected more neurons. That is, volumetric decreases in specific callosal regions in normal adults were found to indicate fewer axons. However, a study of the pre- and postnatal development of the corpus callosum in monkeys (Lamantia & Rakic, 1990) suggested that the primary postnatal developmental change in the corpus callosum is loss of fibers. Thus, the best interpretation of developmental increases in callosal size in older normal children is increased myelination.

BEHAVIORAL STUDIES OF CALLOSAL DEVELOPMENT

Behavioral evidence for increased integration of information between the hemispheres during childhood comes from a variety of different tasks, including those involving visuomotor integration, tactile comparisons, and bimanual coordination. Brizzolara, Ferretti, Brovedani, Casalini, and Sbrana (1994) studied functional development of the corpus callosum using the crossed–uncrossed difference (CUD) in a simple visuomotor reaction time (RT) task as a measure of interhemispheric transfer time (for a review of CUD studies, see Bashore, 1981). Brizzolara et al. tested 171 participants, who were divided into three age groups: 7-, 9-, and 11-year-olds. They found a significant relation between age and CUD. The simple visuomotor RT data reflected a linear relation to age (RT decreasing with age). However, the relation between CUD and age was more asymptotic, with a larger CUD for the youngest group (21.5 msec) and a smaller CUD for the two older groups (5.8 msec and 6.6 msec, respectively). Thus, CUD was found to diminish with age, suggesting a functional consequence of changes in callosal size and myelination.

A number of previous studies have measured the development of callosal functioning using measures of interhemispheric (interhand) transfer of tactile information (Galin, Johnstone, Nakell, & Herron, 1979; O'Leary, 1980; Quinn & Geffen, 1986). Galin et al. found significant group differences for cross-callosal error rate between 3-year-olds and 5-year-olds, with 3-year-olds having a significantly higher error rate in the between-hand condition, that is, when information had to cross the corpus callosum. Quinn and Geffen also found an improvement in interhemispheric transfer of tactile information with age in children between 5 and 11 years. Their data suggest a diminishing rate of change between 9 and 11 years of age, consistent with the CUD data of Brizzolara et al. (1994). These studies of transfer of tactile information again reveal a functional consequence of maturation of the corpus callosum.

Steese-Seda, Brown, and Caetano (1995) used a bimanual coordination test to measure callosal functioning. They found a significant relation between bimanual response time and age. A steeper negative linear regression was found for the younger children (aged 6–9 years) than for the older children (aged 10–13 years), suggesting that an asymptotic curve best describes the relation between bimanual coordination and age. Similar results were reported by Jeeves, Silver, and Milne (1988), who found that 5- to 6-year-old children preformed like acallosals on a bimanual coordination task, whereas 9- to 12-year-olds performed similar to adults. These data suggest that changes in callosal maturation result in improved ability to integrate the visuomotor activity of the two hands.

Merola and Liederman (1985) tested development of interhemispheric independence by comparing performance on two simultaneously presented tachistoscopic letter-naming tasks when both tasks were presented to the same hemisphere (unilateral) and when the tasks were separated between hemispheres (bilateral). These authors demonstrated that 12- and 14-year-old children showed a significant improvement in dual-task performance for bilateral versus unilateral presentations. However, 10-year-old children showed no such performance advantage for bilateral task presentation. Merola and Liederman (1985) concluded that their results reflected an increasing ability with age of the corpus callosum to shield the different information processing in the two hemispheres from interference. Thus, development of the corpus callosum apparently increases the ability of each hemisphere to process information independently, without interference or crosstalk from processing in the other hemisphere.

The callosal myelination data of Yakovlev and Lecours (1967) and the MRI studies of callosal size (Giedd et al., 1996; Pujol et al. 1993; Rajapakse et al., 1996) suggest that callosal maturation continues into the second decade. However, the behavioral studies described previously all seem to indicate that the functional consequences of callosal maturation are beginning to reach asymptote at the beginning of the second decade. It may be that by the beginning of the second decade sufficient callosal development has occurred to sustain maximum performance on the tasks employed in research thus far. More sensitive behavioral tasks may reveal continued changes in interhemispheric transfer or integration of processing.

This study is concerned with the cross-hemispheric integration of visual information. In this research paradigm, two stimuli are presented either unilaterally (both stimuli to one visual field and thus to one hemisphere) or bilaterally (each stimulus to a different visual field and hemisphere). This type of task typically results in a bilateral field advantage (BFA). A BFA is present when a participant responds with greater efficiency (speed or accuracy) when two stimuli to be compared are presented in different visual fields rather than both stimuli in the same visual field. This bilateral advantage in either RT or error rate is a robust finding that is thought to depend on normal callosal function (Banich & Belger, 1990; Berger, 1988; Brown & Jeeves, 1993; Dimond & Beaumont, 1971, 1972; Jeeves & Lamb, 1988; Larson & Brown, 1997; Liederman, Merola, & Martinez, 1985; Ludwig, Jeeves, Norman, & DeWitt, 1993). Several studies have suggested that the BFA increases as task complexity increases (Banich & Belger, 1990; Merola & Liederman, 1990), suggesting that division of early stimulus processing between the hemispheres is particularly beneficial when processing demands are high as long as there is sufficient interhemispheric interaction to allow for an eventual comparison of the results of the separate unilateral processing.

EVOKED POTENTIAL MEASURE OF INTERHEMISPHERIC TRANSMISSION TIME

A measure of the speed of visual sensory information transfer between the cerebral hemispheres can be extracted from visual evoked potentials (EPs) to lateralized visual stimuli (Brown, Bjerke, & Galbraith, 1998; Brown & Jeeves, 1993; Brown, Larson, & Jeeves, 1994; Larson & Brown, 1997; Rugg & Beaumont, 1978; Rugg, Lines, & Milner, 1984; Saron & Davidson, 1989). The P1 and N1 components of the visual EP are, respectively, the first positive wave (at approximately 100 msec poststimulus) and the first negative wave (at approximately 150 msec). These components are generated in the extrastriate visual cortex (P1) and in the inferior parietal and occipitoparietal regions (N1), and they therefore represent early perceptual processing (Clark & Hillyard, 1996; Simpson, Foxe, Vaughan, Mehta, & Schroeder, 1995). When a stimulus occurs in only one visual field, the P1 and N1 components recorded over the ipsilateral (cross-callosal) hemisphere are consistently found to be smaller in amplitude and delayed in latency compared with the same components recorded over the directly stimulated (contralateral) hemisphere. The latency delay (between 10 and 15 msec) has consistently been interpreted as an index of interhemispheric transfer time (IHTT). Brown et al. (1994) reviewed the literature demonstrating the consistency of EP-IHTT findings. This EP method has also been demonstrated to be a reliable method of measuring IHTT (Saron & Davidson, 1989). That the cross-callosal EP (ipsilateral to the visual field of stimulation) is dependent on callosal transfer has been convincingly demonstrated by the absence of the ipsilateral P1 and N1 in recordings from individuals with callosal agenesis (Brown, Jeeves, Dietrich, & Burnison, 1999; Rugg, Milner, & Lines, 1985) and in commissurotomy patients (Brown et al., 1999; Mangun, Luck, Gazzaniga, & Hillyard, 1991). Given that the same absence of ipsilateral P1–N1 occurs in partial callosal agenesis, in which only a posterior portion of the callosum is missing, interhemispheric transfer of the P1–N1 activity must depend on posterior fibers, likely the splenium (Brown et al., 1999). The advantage of using EPs to monitor callosal activity is that it allows the researcher to observe brain activity more directly, as compared with behaviors such as RT (Brown & Jeeves, 1993). EP-IHTT has been found to be an effective way to detect significant group differences in callosal function in a variety of clinical populations (Burnison, Larson, & Brown, 1995; Markee et al., 1996).

Only one previous study measured callosal maturation in normal children using EP-IHTT (Salamy, 1978). Salamy tested 60 healthy participants from ages 2 years to adulthood using EPs to tactile stimulation of the left or right index finger. Salamy found a significant relation between age and IHTT for P1, N1, and P2 (second positive component) for participants ranging from 3.5 years old to 13 years old. This correlation was not significant when Salamy compared participants from ages 10 years to adulthood. Thus, these data also support the notion that callosal transfer speed reaches asymptote around the end of the first decade of life.

This article reports perceptual and electrophysiological correlates of callosal development by observing the visual BFA and simultaneously recorded visual EPs in normal children between 7 and 17 years of age. We expected that EP-IHTT would become faster and that cross-callosal EP amplitude differences would decrease with child development, suggesting more efficient callosal transfer. We also expected that the BFA measured by both RT and error rate would increase progressively with age as a result of more accurate and rapid bilateral comparisons of visual stimuli.

METHOD

Participants

Forty-three children, ranging in age from 7 to 17 years, participated in this study. They were recruited using two methods: a letter sent to the parents of children attending a local parochial school and an advertisement for participation of children placed in a university newspaper. Parents of children who agreed to participate in the study were sent a copy of the informed consent by mail, and an appointment for testing was arranged. Parents were encouraged to be present in a waiting room adjoining the laboratory throughout the testing of each participant. Parental consent was obtained according to American Psychological Association standards. The Institutional Review Board approved all procedures.

Each participant was screened using a comprehensive medical and developmental history questionnaire; participants were also screened for behavioral problems using the Child Behavior Checklist (CBCL; Achenbach & Edelbrock, 1983). Participants were excluded from this study if they had diagnosed learning disabilities, a psychiatric diagnosis, a brain injury that had resulted in loss of consciousness, or any behavioral disorder reflected by elevated scores on the CBCL. Six participants were excluded based on this information: one because of a head injury with loss of consciousness greater than 30 min, another because of a significant reading disability, and four because of elevated scores (*T* scores ≥ 70) on the CBCL. Three additional participants were not included because of unreadable event-related potential (ERP) data (i.e., researchers were unable to detect clear P1–N1 components in the direct-path ERPs). For the purpose of age comparison, participants were divided into three age groups (ages 7–9, $n = 11$; ages 10–12, $n = 10$; and ages 13–17, $n = 13$).

Procedures for the Letter-Matching Task

Participants were tested in two sessions with a break in between. Younger participants (ages 7–9 years) were tested on two separate occasions (with no more than a 2-week break between sessions) to eliminate fatigue and inattention. Participants were randomly assigned to begin testing with either Session 1 or Session 2.

During Session 1, participants performed a letter-matching task in which they were asked to decide whether letters simultaneously flashed on the screen were a "match" or a "nonmatch" (Brown & Jeeves, 1993). The letters tested were *A, a, B,* and *b.* A match consists of two of the same letter, regardless of case (e.g., "A" and "a" are a match). The two letters were located in two of four possible positions in a rectangle surrounding a constantly visible fixation point. The letters were located 2° 19′ of visual angle to the right and left of the fixation point, and 1° 56′ above and below the fixation point. Letters were presented on different trials in one of six possible stimulus configurations: both letters in the right visual field (RVF), both letters in the left visual field (LVF), upper and lower bilateral horizontal presentations, and right-to-left or left-to-right bilateral diagonal presentations. All stimuli were presented on a computer screen for an exposure duration of 200 msec. Each trial was preceded by a warning tone that sounded 500 msec prior to letter onset. The intervals between trials were varied randomly between 1.5 sec and 2.5 sec.

Participants were instructed to press the "M" and "N" keys of a computer keyboard to indicate a match and nonmatch response, respectively. Participants alternated between pressing with the right hand (index finger N and middle finger M) and with the left hand (index finger M and middle finger N). Participants responded to blocks of 48 trials (12 trials each of unilateral LVF, unilateral RVF, bilateral horizontal, and bilateral diagonal). Each participant received four blocks using one hand and four blocks using the other hand, counterbalancing the beginning hand between participants. For each trial, both the RT and the response outcome (correct or incorrect), along with information on the type of trial, were stored in a computer file for later analysis of performance. RTs less than 200 msec or greater than 2 sec were not allowed, and only RTs to correct responses were analyzed.

We calculated RT BFA in a way that adjusted for each individual participant's range of RT variability. Participants with slower and more variable RTs would be likely to have inflated absolute bilateral–unilateral differences, whereas participants with very fast, less variant RTs may have unusually small BFAs. Thus, RT BFA was expressed as a within-subjects standard score: (unilateral RT – bilateral RT)/standard deviation of RTs for all trials for that participant. This standardized statistic helped ensure that the test of age-related changes in the bilateral processing advantage was not contaminated by the overall speed of each particular participant's RT. For error rate (percentage of incorrect trials), the difference between unilateral and bilateral trials was computed for each participant as a measure of relative BFA for response accuracy.

The second testing session included the following neuropsychological measures. Each participant was administered an adapted version of the Edinburgh handedness test. Handedness was assessed as right or left with a mean score of 5 (out of 7) or more in either direction. The participants were also given four subtests from the Wechsler Intelligence Scale for Children–Revised (WISC-R; Wechsler, 1974; Vocabulary, Similarities, Block Design, and Picture Arrangement), from which an estimated full scale IQ (FSIQ) was obtained using the calculation method described by Sattler (1992). All of the participants were also assessed using the CBCL (Achenbach & Edelbrock, 1983).

Evoked Potential Recording

While participants performed the letter detection task, evoked electroencephalogram (EEG) potentials to letter presentation were recorded simultaneously using methods described earlier (e.g., Brown & Jeeves, 1993). Electrodes were attached to midline occipital (Oz), to right (RtC) and left (LtC) central loci (midway between vertex [Cz] and the interaural line over each hemisphere), and to right (RtP) and left (LtP) parietal loci. Because the parietal electrodes were approximately over the scalp locus of the maximum voltage for both P1 and N1, and because the central electrodes were on the periphery of the voltage field, responses from the parietal electrodes are reported herein. Recordings were referenced to linked earlobe electrodes. In addition, electrodes were attached both above and at the outer canthus of the right eye for bipolar recording of eye movements. Participants were grounded at Cz. EEG records began 140 msec prior to stimulus onset and extended 500 msec poststimulus (2 msec per sample). The EEGs were amplified 20,000 times and filtered 0.1 Hz to 100 Hz (3 dB down).

EPs were recorded for each trial involving unilateral visual field presentations. These potentials from each electrode were averaged separately for LVF and RVF trials. Only trials in which an individual gave a correct response were included in the averages. P1 and N1 components were visually identified in the EPs of each participant, and the amplitude and latency of these components were recorded for each electrode and stimulus condition. Individual trials were considered artifacts and were eliminated from EP averages if the overall amplitude exceeded a preset window.

EP-IHTTs were calculated separately for P1 and N1 latencies. EP-IHTT is the difference in latency between direct responses (LVF to right hemisphere or RVF to left hemisphere) and the cross-callosal responses (LVF to left hemisphere or RVF to right hemisphere). EP amplitude was measured from peak to peak (P1 to N1). The cross-callosal decrement in amplitude (i.e., interhemispheric transmission of amplitude) was calculated in the same manner as IHTT using the P1–N1 peak-to-peak amplitude rather than component latencies.

RESULTS

Descriptive statistics by age group are presented in Table 1. Initial analyses showed that there were no significant differences between the three groups on any of the demographic variables, including gender, handedness, and estimated FSIQ. There were also no differences in mean CBCL scores.

TABLE 1
Demographic Data

Variable and Age Group	*7 to 9 Years*	*10 to 12 Years*	*13 to 17 Years*
Total	11.00	10.00	13.00
Age in years			
M	7.91	11.10	14.23
SD	0.94	0.99	1.36
Handedness (number of participants)			
Left	3.00	1.00	2.00
Right	8.00	9.00	10.00
Mixed	0.00	0.00	1.00
Gender (number of participants)			
Men	6.00	5.00	9.00
Women	5.00	5.00	4.00
Estimated FSIQ			
M	125.47	125.29	123.02
SD	8.94	9.73	12.44
CBCL Total *T* Score			
M	46.27	48.00	48.77
SD	5.26	5.73	11.12

Note. FSIQ = full scale IQ; CBCL = Child Behavior Checklist (Achenbach & Edelbrock, 1983).

BFA RT

RT data can be seen in Table 2. To confirm the existence of a clear BFA within each age group, a unilateral versus bilateral analysis of variance (ANOVA) was carried out for each age group. Results revealed that bilateral RTs were significantly faster than unilateral RTs in both of the older groups: 13- to 17-year-olds, $F(1, 12) = 13.46, p < .003$; 10- to 12-year-olds, $F(1, 9) = 25.72, p = .001$. For the younger group (7–9-year-olds), there was only a trend toward faster bilateral RTs, $F(1, 10) = 2.70, p = .132$. These data indicate a somewhat less clear BFA in the youngest group compared to the two older groups.

To test this developmental trend in BFA for RT, the difference between unilateral and bilateral trials in RT for each participant was divided by the participant's intertrial RT standard deviation ([unilateral – bilateral]/standard deviation). Mean BFAs for each group can be seen in Figure 1. BFAs were tested in a one-way ANOVA by group. There was a significant difference between the three groups in the expected direction, $F(2, 31) = 2.74, p < .04$ (one-tailed), supporting the hypothesis of increased BFA for RT with age. The youngest group differed significantly from the middle age group, $F(1, 19) = 5.32, p < .04$ (two-tailed), but the two older groups did not differ from each other, $F(1, 21) = 0.83$, *ns*.

The relation between RT BFA and age was also tested by regression methods. Because the BFA ratio can change either by changes in unilateral or bilateral RTs, the age regression was first calculated separately for unilateral and bilateral RTs. Both were significant, although the correlation was slightly stronger for bilateral RTs: bilateral $r(32) = -.451, p < .02$; unilateral $r(32) = -.392, p < .05$. Moreover, the partial correlation of age and bilateral RTs, controlling for unilateral RTs, was still significant, $r(32) = -.405, p < .05$. Thus, the RT for bilateral letter comparisons was signifi-

TABLE 2
Bilateral Field Advantage for Reaction Time and Error Rate by Group

	Unilateral		*Bilateral*	
	M	*SD*	*M*	*SD*
Reaction time (msec)				
Group 1	1,129	291.62	1,105	264.38
Group 2	949	187.73	898	180.64***
Group 3	876	167.46	837	161.50**
Error rate (% incorrect)				
Group 1	20	0.12	18	0.17
Group 2	13	0.05	10	0.03*
Group 3	14	0.11	10	0.12**

*Bilateral advantage, $p < .05$. **Bilateral advantage, $p < .01$. ***Bilateral advantage, $p < .001$.

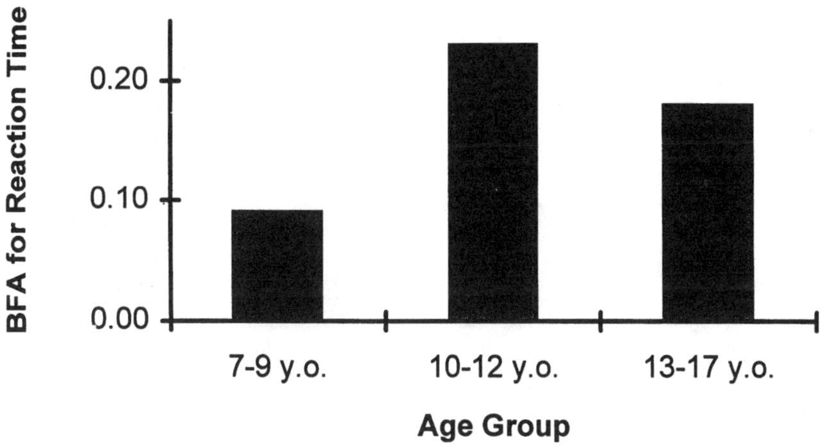

FIGURE 1 Group mean bilateral field advantage for reaction time (RT) in standard units ([unilateral RT – bilateral RT]/overall RT standard deviation). *Note.* BFA = bilateral field advantage; y.o. = years old.

cantly related to age, even when controlling for age-related changes in RT for unilateral letter matching.

BFA Error Rate

Error data for the three groups can also be seen in Table 2. To confirm the existence of a clear BFA for error rate within each age group, a unilateral versus bilateral ANOVA was carried out for each age group. Results revealed that there were significantly fewer errors for bilateral than for unilateral trials in both of the older groups: oldest group, $F(1, 12) = 15.44, p < .002$; middle group, $F(1, 9) = 5.21, p = .048$. In the younger group, the difference in errors between bilateral and unilateral trials was not significant, $F(1, 10) = 0.65$, *ns*. Detection of a significant BFA in errors for the two older groups, but not for the youngest group, again indicates a less clear bilateral advantage in the youngest group.

To test for a developmental trend, the BFA for error rate (unilateral – bilateral) was tested in a one-way ANOVA by group. The difference between groups was not significant, $F(2, 31) = 0.47$, *ns,* suggesting that although there was a significant BFA for error rate in both of the older groups, but not in the youngest group, the group differences in BFA were not great enough to support the predicted developmental trajectory (see Figure 2 for group mean BFA error).

The relation between BFA error and age was further explored using regression methods. Both unilateral and bilateral errors were significantly correlated with age: bilateral, $r(32) = -.356, p < .04$; unilateral, $r(32) = -.335, p < .06$. However, in the

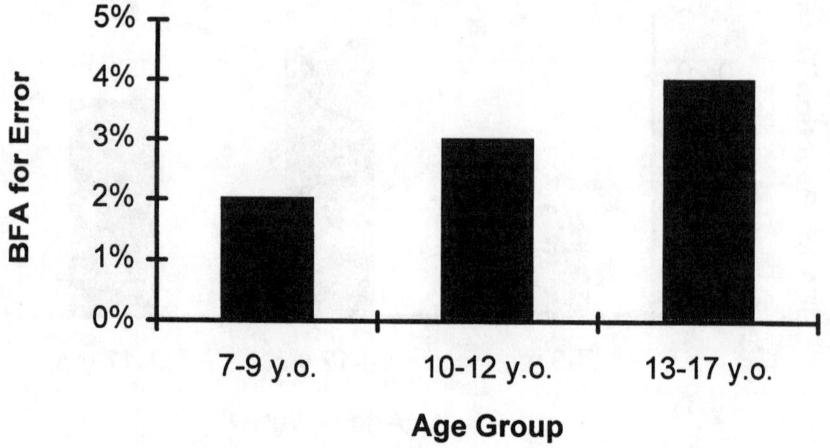

FIGURE 2 Group mean bilateral field advantage for error rate (unilateral % error – bilateral % error). *Note.* BFA = bilateral field advantage; y.o. = years old.

case of errors, the partial correlation of age and bilateral errors controlling for unilateral errors was not significant, $r(32) = -.134$, *ns*.

EP-IHTT

Across-subject mean EPs for each of the three groups can be seen in Figure 3. EP latencies were first analyzed to confirm the existence of a reliable IHTT for both P1 and N1 for each group. The results of these analyses can be seen in Table 3. There was a clear and significant IHTT for both P1 and N1 for all three groups reflected in the interaction between hemisphere and visual field. The only exception was a trend for the P1 component in the middle group (which would be significant using a one-tailed analysis). N1 and P1 IHTT means for each group can be seen in Figure 4.

Previous research with adults in our laboratory had suggested that, at least for the N1 component, EP-IHTT was faster from the right-to-left hemisphere than from the left-to-right hemisphere (Brown et al., 1994). Thus, this difference was tested for the N1 component across all participants. Although the difference in mean N1-IHTT was in the same direction as previously described (i.e., N1-IHTT right-to-left = 13.2 msec; left-to-right = 17.9 msec), the difference was not statistically significant in this sample of children, $t(32) = 0.68$, *ns*.

To detect a developmental trend in IHTT, group differences in the calculated IHTT for both P1 and N1 were tested in separate ANOVAs. There was no P1-IHTT difference between groups. $F(2, 31) = 0.10$, *ns*. However, there was a trend in the predicted direction for the N1 component, $F(2, 31) = 1.97, p = .078$ (one-tailed), with the two older groups having shorter N1-IHTT than the youngest group.

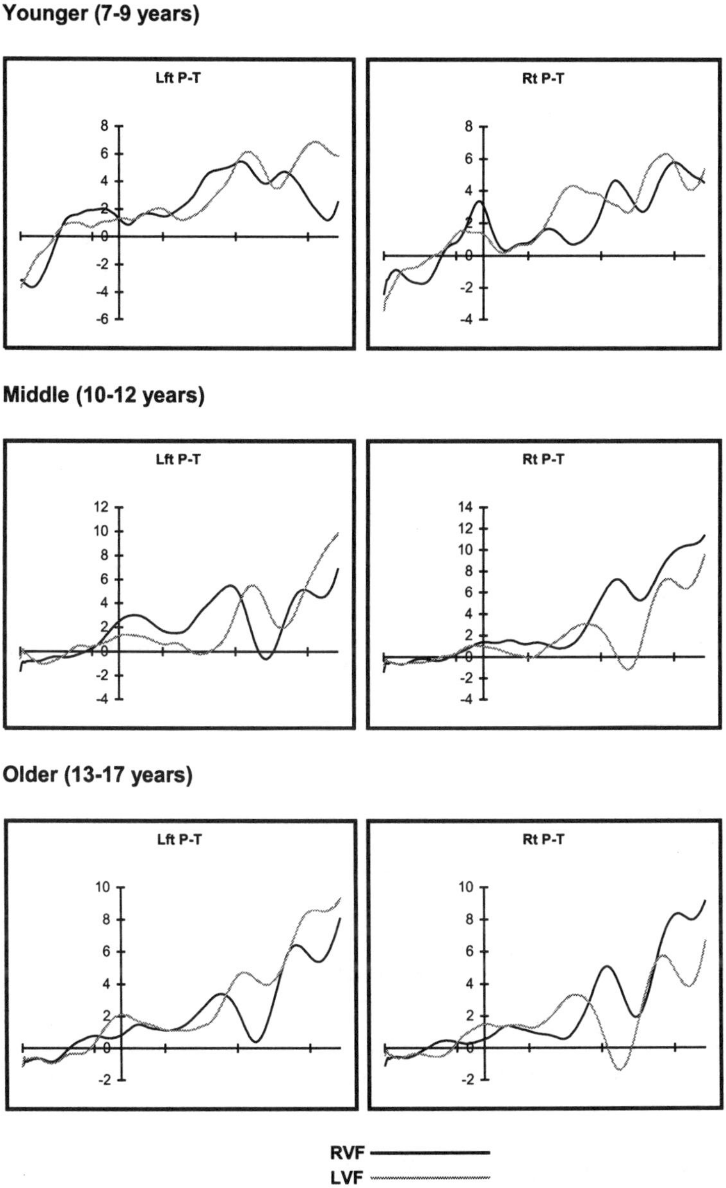

FIGURE 3 Group mean evoked potentials for the left (light lines) and right (dark lines) visual fields recorded from the left (Lft P-T) and right (Rt P-T) parietal-temporal electrode loci. Stimulus onset is at the vertical line, with tick marks every 100 msec. The vertical scale is in microvolts. *Note.* RVF = right visual field; LVF = left visual field.

TABLE 3
Interhemispheric Transmission Time Analysis of Variance Results for P1 and N1 by Group

	VF		*HM*		*VF* × *HM*	
	F	*p*	*F*	*p*	*F*	*p*
P1						
Group 1	0.03	*ns*	1.65	*ns*	17.35	.002
Group 2	2.04	*ns*	0.14	*ns*	4.49	.072
Group 3	0.04	*ns*	1.91	*ns*	21.32	.001
N1						
Group 1	0.01	*ns*	0.59	*ns*	16.16	.002
Group 2	0.01	*ns*	0.69	*ns*	6.22	.041
Group 3	0.01	*ns*	0.31	*ns*	39.35	.000

Note. P1 = first positive wave; N1 = first negative wave; VF = visual field; HM = hemisphere; VF × HM = Visual Field × Hemisphere interaction.

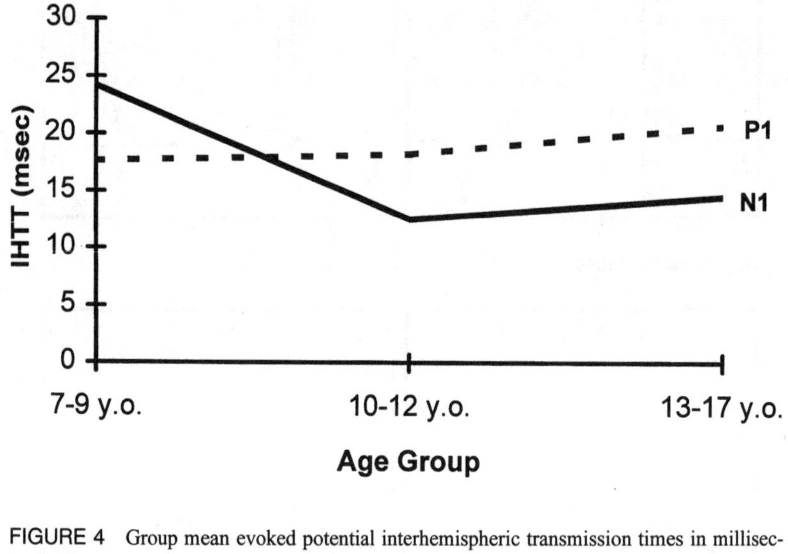

FIGURE 4 Group mean evoked potential interhemispheric transmission times in milliseconds for P1 (dashed line) and N1 (solid line). *Note.* IHTT = interhemispheric transmission time; y.o. = years old.

Because the group difference in EP-IHTT for the N1 component showed some evidence of a developmental trend, the relation between N1-IHTT and age was further evaluated using regression methods. First, N1 latency for both direct-path (e.g., LVF to right hemisphere) and cross-callosal (e.g., LVF to left hemisphere) were found to be significantly correlated with age: direct, $r(32) = -.408$, $p < .02$; cross-callosal, $r(32) = -.460$, $p < .01$. For exploring correlations between N1-IHTT and age, two participants with negative N1-IHTTs were eliminated (a negative IHTT is physiologically impossible and therefore must represent a misidentification of the N1 component in the EPs of one or the other hemisphere). However, the correlation between age and N1-IHTT remained nonsignificant, $r(30) = -.237, p = .171$. Separate correlations between age and right-to-left versus left-to-right N1-IHTT yielded a nearly significant correlation for right-to-left, $r(30) = -.347, p = .071$, but a nonsignificant trend for left-to-right, $r(30) = .240, p = .179$.

Finally, the correlation between N1-IHTT and RT BFA was tested. This correlation was not significant, $r(30) = -.181$, *ns*. The correlation between RT BFA and N1-IHTT for the different directions of interhemispheric transmission was strongest for the right-to-left direction of transmission: right-to-left, $r(30) = -.258, p = .141$; left-to-right, $r(30) = .004$, *ns*.

Evoked Potential Interhemispheric Transfer Amplitude

Lastly, the data were analyzed (by group) for differences in cross-hemispheric decrements in EP amplitude. A visual field-by-hemisphere ANOVA of the P1–N1 peak-to-peak amplitude for each group was done. The interaction of visual field and hemisphere was not significant for any of the three groups. Because the interhemispheric amplitude decrement was not significant for any group, no further analyses were performed on this variable.

DISCUSSION

In summary, it was predicted that developmental changes in myelination of the corpus callosum over the late childhood and early adolescent span would result in larger bilateral advantages in RT and error rate, as well as faster EP-IHTT. Age-related changes in the BFA were significant and in the predicted direction for the RT BFA, and they were in the expected direction, but not significant, for error rate. EP-IHTT for the N1 component became shorter with age, as predicted, but this was only a trend. Thus, the hypothesis of age-related decrease in EP-IHTT could be supported with only marginal statistical confidence. P1-IHTT did not change with age in these participants.

Age changes in both the RT and error rate BFAs were in the same direction, suggesting increasingly fast and accurate bilateral visual field letter comparisons, relative to comparisons made within a single visual field (unilateral). This finding rules out the possibility that the significant increase in RT BFA was due to a shifting speed–accuracy trade-off. If tactical choices regarding speed versus accuracy had shifted, the increasing RT BFA would have been accompanied by a greater bilateral disadvantage (unilateral advantage) in error rate, which did not occur. These results emphasize why both speed and accuracy need to be analyzed in studies of the BFA.

A review of several studies of developmental changes in interhemispheric interactions using tactile, motor, and visual tasks (Brizzolara et al., 1994; Galin et al., 1979; Jeeves et al., 1988; Merola & Liederman, 1985; Quinn & Geffen, 1986; Steese-Seda et al., 1995) indicates that all seemed to suggest that developmental trends reached asymptote around the beginning of the second decade. However, the myelination data from postmortem examinations (Yakovlev & Lecours, 1967) and the MRI evidence (Giedd et al., 1996; Pujol et al., 1993; Rajapakse et al., 1996) suggest a longer process of callosal development. One explanation introduced earlier was test sensitivity; that is, the various tests used were not sensitive to the implications of further callosal development beyond the first decade.

Recent work by Brown et al. (1999) demonstrated that adults with complete callosal agenesis could do the same bilateral letter-matching task used with children in this research. Some acallosals even showed a significant bilateral advantage. Examination of the MRIs of all of these acallosal participants revealed an intact anterior commissure, suggesting that in these adult acallosals, the anterior commissure was sufficient to mediate bilateral comparisons. However, a more complex visual pattern-matching task showed clear bilateral matching deficits in acallosals. It was concluded that the complexity of the visual material may determine the degree to which a callosal function deficit can be detected. In this light, the developmental data of this study may suggest that the immature corpus callosum was the predominant means of interhemispheric interactions in bilateral letter matching for the younger group, but that sometime around or after the age of 10, letter processing becomes sufficiently easy (i.e., automated and readily encoded) to allow for interhemispheric transfer to occur via the anterior commissure. If this is the case, then a task requiring interhemispheric matching of stimuli more complex than letters would be required to detect the functional significance of continued callosal development beyond the onset of the second decade.

Banich and Belger (1990) have rightly argued that a bilateral advantage measured from the stimulus paradigm used in this research suffers from confounding, in that each hemisphere must process only one letter on bilateral trials, whereas each hemisphere must process two letters in unilateral trials (with no stimulus at all appearing to the opposite hemisphere). However, the requirement of simultaneous recording of EPs to unilateral visual field presentations did not allow us to use alternative paradigms suggested by Banich and Belger. Nevertheless, because each hemisphere improved with age in a similar manner in its ability to simultaneously process two letters, the increasing bilateral advantage must be due to a greater increase in the ability to integrate bilateral processing as the corpus callosum myelinates and matures.

The significant age-related change in BFA demonstrated in this study suggests that callosal myelination has functional consequences for the interhemispheric interactions necessary to compare information in the two visual fields. There are two alternative interpretations of this age-related change in callosal function. First, callosal maturation may allow greater independence of processing within each hemisphere. This is the process that Kinsbourne (1970) termed *shielding.* Banich and Belger (1990) argued for the importance of shielding, suggesting that a bilateral advantage occurs when the same hemisphere must simultaneously process two items of complex information. When the stimuli are presented separately, one to each hemisphere, less interference occurs, so that each stimulus can be preprocessed more efficiently prior to interhemispheric comparison. Evidence supporting this theory of BFA comes from the demonstration that as stimulus complexity becomes greater, the BFA increases (Banich & Belger, 1990). Merola and Liederman (1985) also showed that, in older children, interference between stimuli was diminished by separating stimuli into the two visual fields. However, younger children did not gain an advantage from such stimulus separation. Therefore, according to this theory, increased callosal function in children led to an increased BFA by diminishing interference in the preprocessing of the two letter stimuli, which must be compared in a later stage of processing. At one level, this theory of age-related changes is somewhat counterintuitive, in that the hemispheres would be hypothesized to process information more independently as the corpus callosum matures. However, if one assumes that increased callosal maturation allows for better regulation of processing and reduced crosstalk between the hemispheres, then the shielding theory of the consequences of callosal development for the BFA has merit.

An alternative, although not mutually exclusive, interpretation is that the BFA increases in child development because information is more quickly and accurately transmitted between the hemispheres. This interpretation would be consistent with the concept of "sharing," as described by Kinsbourne (1970). Although the change in EP-IHTT with age was not significant in this study, the group difference in mean EP-IHTT was substantial enough to suggest that information may be more rapidly transmitted between the hemispheres as children mature. Increasingly fast IHTT with age would lend some support to the hypothesis that the increased BFA with child development represents more efficient bilateral sharing of the information necessary for bilateral letter comparisons. However, BFA and EP-IHTT were not found to be correlated; therefore, these measures would appear to represent different aspects of callosal function.

As described previously, it is clear that the ipsilateral P1–N1 to a lateralized visual stimulus is dependent on callosal transfer, because it is absent in recordings from individuals with callosal agenesis (Brown et al., 1999; Rugg et al., 1985) and in commissurotomy patients (Brown et al., 1999; Mangun et al., 1991). Similar absence of ipsilateral P1–N1 in individuals with partial callosal agenesis points to the posterior corpus callosum (likely the splenium) as the mediating structure (Brown et al., 1999). Both the P1 and N1 have scalp-field amplitude maximal over occipital-parietal margin (Saron, Foxe, Simpson, & Vaughan, in press), suggesting occipitoparietal loci for the P1–N1 generators. This is consistent with attempts at 3-D source localization of these EP components (Clark & Hillyard, 1996; Simpson et al., 1995). Thus, the EP-IHTT examined in this research is a direct reflection of visual sensory transfer between extrastriate cortex in each hemisphere.

It is unlikely that the critical channel for the BFA is the splenium, the portion of the callosum that carries the visual P1–N1 activity by which EP-IHTT is measured. However, the EP-IHTT provides the best available index of a participant's relative callosal transfer speed in the corpus callosum. Thus, in a developmental context, the EP-IHTT is a reasonable (although indirect) index of the relative IHTT for the corpus callosum as a whole for a particular participant.

Although the group difference in mean N1-IHTT between the youngest group and the next older group was nearly 10 msec (see Figure 1), the age-related difference was only marginally statistically significant. Age-related changes in EP-IHTT were not detectable for the P1 component. The P1 component to our lateralized letter stimuli recorded from posterior parietal scalp loci has proven consistently small and difficult to reliably identify in both adults (Brown & Jeeves, 1993; Brown et al., 1994) and children (this study). The N1 component is much larger and can be more reliably measured, and thus it represents the most reliable index of EP-IHTT.

These EP-IHTT results, although not significant, are consistent in direction with the results of Salamy (1978), who used tactile rather than visual stimuli. Salamy found a significant increase in the speed of interhemispheric transmission in participants between 3.5 and 10 years, whereas the lesser change in speed of transmission occurring between the ages of 10 and 20 was not significant. Tactile transmission time for both P1 and N1 diminished by approximately 16 msec between the ages of 3.5 and 20 years. Why this age effect was not more significant in this research is uncertain. The differences in statistical outcomes between our experiment and that of Salamy may reflect any or all of the following: (a) signal-to-noise differences in tactile versus visual EPs, (b) differences in recording methods (e.g., Salamy used the vertex as a common reference and more anterior parietal electrodes, whereas we used linked earlobes and more posterior parietal recording sites), or (c) differences in number of participants (Salamy tested 60 children).

In summary, the overall congruence of the BFA and EP-IHTT data is consistent with either stage of a two-stage model of the bilateral advantage in comparing two visual stimuli: (a) an early stage of stimulus preprocessing in which speed and accuracy are enhanced by hemispherically separate stimulus processing, and (b) a later stage of interhemispheric integration of processing that is enhanced by faster and more efficient interhemispheric transmission. The corpus callosum contains multiple interhemispheric channels, involving perceptual, motor, and other forms of information. Faster, more efficient callosal transfer (indexed by EP-IHTT) could potentially operate over one or several of such channels to facilitate either stage—either by enhancing modulatory influences to decrease interference and crosstalk to allow more independent processing or by speeding the rate of interhemispheric transfer.

REFERENCES

Aboitiz, F. (1992). Brain connections: Interhemispheric fiber systems and anatomical brain asymmetries in humans. *Biological Research, 26,* 51–61.

Aboitiz, F., Scheibel, A. B., Fisher, R. S., & Zaidel, E. (1992). Fiber composition of the human corpus callosum. *Brain Research, 598,* 143–153.

Achenbach, T. M., & Edelbrock, C. (1983). *Manual for the Child Behavior Checklist and Revised Child Behavior Profile.* Burlington, VT: University of Vermont, Department of Psychiatry.

Banich, M. T., & Belger, A. (1990). Interhemispheric interaction: How do the hemispheres divide and conquer a task? *Cortex, 26,* 77–94.

Barkovich, A. J., & Maroldo, T. V. (1993). Magnetic resonance imaging of normal and abnormal brain development. *Topics in Magnetic Resonance Imaging, 5,* 96–122.

Bashore, T. R. (1981). Vocal and manual reaction time estimates of interhemispheric transmission time. *Psychological Bulletin, 89,* 352–368.

Baumgardner, T. L., Singer, H. S., Denckla, M. B., Rubin, M. A., Abrams, M. T., Colli, M. J., & Reiss, A. L. (1996). Corpus callosum morphology in children with Tourette syndrome and attention deficit hyperactivity disorder. *Neurology, 47,* 477–482.

Belmonte, M., Egaas, B., Townsend, J., & Courchesne, E. (1995). NMR intensity of corpus callosum differs with age but not with diagnosis of autism. *Neuroreport, 6,* 1253–1256.

Berger, J.-M. (1988). Interhemispheric cooperation and activation in integration of verbal information. *Behavioural Brain Research, 29,* 193–200.

Bodensteiner, J., Schaefer, G., Breeding, L., & Cowan, L. (1994). Hypoplasia of the corpus callosum: A study of 445 consecutive MRI scans. *Journal of Child Neurology, 9,* 47–49.

Brizzolara, D., Ferretti, G., Brovedani, P., Casalini, C., & Sbrana, B. (1994). Is interhemispheric transfer time related to age? A developmental study. *Behavioural Brain Research, 64,* 179–184.

Brown, W. S., Bjerke, M. D., & Galbraith, G. C. (1998). Interhemispheric transfer in normals and acallosals: Latency adjusted evoked potential averaging. *Cortex, 34,* 677–692.

Brown, W. S., & Jeeves, M. A. (1993). Bilateral visual field processing and evoked potential interhemispheric transmission time. *Neuropsychologia, 31,* 1267–1281.

Brown, W. S., Jeeves, M. A., Dietrich, R., & Burnison, D. S. (1999). Bilateral field advantage and evoked potential interhemispheric transmission in commissurotomy and callosal agenesis. *Neuropsychologia, 37,* 1165–1180.

Brown, W., Larson, E., & Jeeves, M. (1994). Directional asymmetries in interhemispheric transmission time: Evidence from visual evoked potentials. *Neuropsychologia, 32,* 439–448.

Burnison, D. S., Larson, E. B., & Brown, W. S. (1995). Evoked potential interhemispheric transmission and the bilateral field advantage in multiple sclerosis [Abstract]. *Journal of the International Neuropsychological Society, 1,* 182.

Clark, V. P., & Hillyard, S. A. (1996). Spatial selective attention affects early extrastriate but not striate components of the visual evoked potential. *Journal of Cognitive Neuroscience, 8,* 387–402.

David, A. (1993). Callosal transfer in schizophrenia: Too much or too little? *Journal of Abnormal Psychology, 102,* 573–579.

Dimond, S., & Beaumont, G. (1971). Use of two cerebral hemispheres to increase brain capacity. *Nature, 232,* 270–271.

Dimond, S., & Beaumont, G. (1972). Processing in perceptual integration between and within the cerebral hemispheres. *British Journal of Psychology, 63,* 509–514.

Galin, D., Johnstone, J., Nakell, L., & Herron, J. (1979). Development of the capacity for tactile information transfer between hemispheres in normal children. *Science, 204,* 1330–1332.

Giedd, J. N., Rumsey, J. M., Castellanos, F. X., Rajapakse, J. C., Kaysen, D., Vaituzis, A. C., Vauss, Y. C., Hamburger, S. D., & Rapoport, J. L. (1996). A quantitative MRI study of the corpus callosum in children and adolescents. *Brain Research: Developmental Brain Research, 91,* 274–280.

Hynd, G. W., Semrud-Clikeman, M., Lorys, A. R., Novey, E. S., & Eliopulos, D. (1990). Brain morphology in developmental dyslexia and attention deficit disorder/hyperactivity. *Archives of Neurology, 47,* 919–926.

Hynd, G., Semrud-Clikeman, M., Lorys, A., Novey, E., Eliopulos D., & Lyytinen, H. (1991). Corpus callosum morphology in attention deficit-hyperactivity disorder: Morphometric analysis of MRI. *Journal of Learning Disabilities, 24,* 141–146.

Jeeves, M. A., & Lamb, A. (1988). Cerebral asymmetries and interhemispheric processes. *Behavioural Brain Research, 29,* 211–223.

Jeeves, M. A., Silver, P. H., & Milne, A. B. (1988). Role of the corpus callosum in the development of a bimanual motor skill. *Developmental Neuropsychology, 4,* 305–323.

Kinsbourne, M. (1970). The cerebral basis of lateral asymmetries in attention. *Acta Psychologica, 33,* 193–201.

Lamantia, A. S., & Rakic, P. (1990). Axon overproduction and elimination in the corpus callosum of the developing rhesus monkey. *Journal of Neuroscience, 10,* 2156–2175.

Larson, E. B., & Brown, W. S. (1997). Bilateral field interactions, hemispheric specialization and evoked potential interhemispheric transmission time. *Neuropsychologia, 35,* 573–581.

Liederman, J., Merola, J., & Martinez, S. (1985). Inter-hemispheric collaboration in response to simultaneous bilateral input. *Neuropsychologia, 23,* 673–683.

Ludwig, T. E., Jeeves, M. A., Norman, W. D., & DeWitt, R. (1993). The bilateral field advantage on a letter-matching task. *Cortex, 29,* 691–713.

Mangun, G. R., Luck, S. J., Gazzaniga, M. S., & Hillyard, S. A. (1991). Electrophysiological measures of interhemispheric transfer of visual information: Studies of split-brain patients [Abstract]. *Society for Neuroscience, 17,* 340.4.

Markee, T., Brown, W. S., Moore, L. H., & Theberge, D. C. (1996). Callosal function in dyslexia: Evoked potential interhemispheric transfer time and bilateral field advantage. *Developmental Neuropsychology, 12,* 409–428.

Merola, J. L., & Liederman, J. (1985). Developmental changes in hemispheric independence. *Child Development, 56,* 1184–1194.

Merola, J., & Liederman, J. (1990). The extent to which between-hemisphere division of inputs improves performance depends upon task difficulty. *Journal of Clinical and Experimental Neuropsychology, 10,* 69.

Moore, L., Brown, W. S., Markee, T., Theberge, D., & Zvi, J. (1995). Bimanual coordination in dyslexic adults. *Neuropsychologia, 33,* 781–793.

Moore, L., Brown, W. S., Markee, T., Theberge, D., & Zvi, J. (1996). Callosal transfer of finger localization information in phonologically dyslexic adults. *Cortex, 32,* 311–322.

Njiokiktjien, C., de Sonneville, L., & Vaal, J. (1994). Callosal size in children with learning disabilities. *Behavioural Brain Research, 64,* 213–218.

O'Leary, D. S. (1980). A developmental study of interhemispheric transfer in children aged five to ten. *Child Development, 51,* 743–750.

Ono, J., Kodaka, R., Imai, K., Itagaki, Y., Tanaka, J., Inui, K., Nagai, T., Sakurai, K., Harada, K., & Okada, S. (1993). Evaluation of myelination by means of the T2 value on magnetic resonance imaging. *Brain and Development, 15,* 433–438.

Pujol, J., Vendrell, P., Junqué, C., Martì-Vilalta, J., & Capdevila, A. (1993). When does human brain development end? Evidence of corpus callosum growth up to adulthood. *Annals of Neurology, 34,* 71–75.

Quinn, K., & Geffen, G. (1986). The development of tactile transfer of information. *Neuropsychologia, 24,* 793–804.

Raine, A., Harrison, G., Reynolds, G., Sheard, C., Cooper, J., & Medley, I. (1990). Structural and functional characteristics of the corpus callosum in schizophrenics, psychiatric controls, and normal controls. *Archives of General Psychiatry, 47,* 1060–1064.

Rajapakse J. C., Giedd, J. N., Rumsey, J. M., Vaituzis, A. C., Hamburger, S. D., & Rapoport, J. L. (1996). Regional MRI measurements of the corpus callosum: A methodological and developmental study. *Brain and Development, 18,* 379–388.

Rugg, M. D., & Beaumont, J. G. (1978). Interhemispheric asymmetries in the visual evoked response: Effects of stimulus lateralisation and task. *Biological Psychology, 6,* 283–292.

Rugg, M. D., Lines, C. R., & Milner, A. D. (1984). Visual evoked potentials to lateralized visual stimuli and the measurement of interhemispheric transmission time. *Neuropsychologia, 22,* 215–225.

Rugg, M. D., Milner, A. D., & Lines, C. R. (1985). Visual evoked potentials to lateralised stimuli in two cases of callosal agenesis. *Journal of Neurology, Neurosurgery, and Psychiatry, 48,* 367–373.

Salamy, A. (1978). Commissural transmission: Maturational changes in humans. *Science, 22,* 1409–1411.

Saron, C. D., & Davidson, R. J. (1989). Visual evoked potential measures of interhemispheric transfer time in humans. *Behavioral Neuroscience, 103,* 1115–1138.

Saron, C. D., Foxe, J. J., Simpson, G. V., & Vaughan, H. G., Jr. (in press). Electrophysiological indices of intra- and interhemispheric visuomotor interaction. In E. Zaidel, M. Iacoboni, & A. Pascual-Leon (Eds.), *The corpus callosum in sensory motor integration: Individual differences and clinical applications.* Cambridge, MA: MIT Press.

Sattler, J. M. (1992). *Assessment of children* (Rev. ed.). San Diego, CA: Author.

Simpson, G. V., Foxe, J. J., Vaughan, J. G., Mehta, A. D., & Schroeder, C. E. (1995). Integration of electrophysiological source analyses, MRI and animal models in the study of visual processing and attention. *Electroencephalography and Clinical Neurology,* (Suppl. 44), 76–92.

Steese-Seda, D., Brown, W. S., & Caetano, C. (1995). Development of visuomotor coordination in school-age children: The bimanual coordination test. *Developmental Neuropsychology, 11,* 181–199.

Wechsler, D. (1974). *The Wechsler Intelligence Scale for Children–Revised.* New York: Psychological Corporation.

Yakovlev, P. I., & Lecours, A. R. (1967). The myelogenetic cycles of regional maturation of the brain. In A. Minkowski (Ed.), *Regional development of the brain in early life* (pp. 3–70). Oxford, England: Blackwell.

DEVELOPMENTAL NEUROPSYCHOLOGY, *18*(1), 33–51

Interhemispheric Interaction During Childhood: I. Neurologically Intact Children

Marie T. Banich
The Beckman Institute
Department of Psychology
University of Illinois at Urbana–Champaign

Alessandra M. Passarotti
Department of Cognitive Sciences
University of California at San Diego

Dana Janes
The Beckman Institute
Department of Psychology
University of Illinois at Urbana–Champaign

This study examined the development of interaction between the hemispheres as a function of computational complexity (Banich & Belger, 1990; Belger & Banich, 1992) in 24 children aged 6.5 to 14 years. Participants performed 2 tasks: a less complex physical-identity task and a more complex name-identity task. Children, like adults, exhibit an across-hemisphere advantage on the computationally more complex name-identity task, and neither a within- nor an across-hemisphere advantage for the computationally less complex physical-identity task. Correlations indicated that the younger the child, (a) the greater the size of the within-hemisphere advantage on the less complex task, (b) the greater the size of the across-hemisphere advantage on the more complex task, and (c) the poorer the ability to ignore attentionally distracting information in a selective attention paradigm. These results suggest that interhemispheric interaction in children, like that in adults, serves to deal with the heightened processing demands imposed by increased computational complexity.

Requests for reprints should be sent to Marie T. Banich, Department of Psychology, University of Colorado at Boulder, UCB 345, Boulder, CO 80309. E-mail: mbanich@psych.colorado.edu

In this article, we examine whether functional interaction between the hemispheres changes during childhood. This question is of interest because the corpus callosum, the nerve fiber tract providing cortical connections between the hemispheres and the major conduit for interhemispheric interaction, continues to myelinate up until the early adult years (Giedd et al., 1996). Myelination is the process whereby glial cells form a fatty insulating sheath around axons, allowing for faster conduction of neural impulses. Increased myelination of the callosum throughout childhood increases the speed of neural transmission and implies that the efficiency of interhemispheric communication increases during this developmental period.

A number of different approaches have been taken to examine whether the functional connectivity between the hemispheres indeed increases with age (for a review, see Hagelthorn, Brown, Amano, & Asarnow, this issue). Some researchers have examined whether the speed of callosal transmission decreases with age. For example, a subset of investigators examined whether estimates of interhemispheric transfer time, as derived from behavioral measures (e.g., Brizzolara, Ferretti, Brovendani, Casalini, & Sbrana, 1994; Ratinckx, Brysbaert, & d'Ydewalle, 1997) or evoked potentials (e.g., Hagelthorn et al., this issue; Salamy, 1978) to simple stimuli such as light flashes, change with age. Others used behavioral tasks to examine developmental changes in the ability to compare stimuli across the hemispheres (e.g., O'Leary, 1980; Quinn & Geffen, 1986). Still others examined the degree to which the hemispheres can work independently of one another in childhood, from both a cross-sectional (Merola & Liederman, 1985) and a longitudinal (e.g., Liederman, Merola, & Hoffman, 1986) perspective. The results of these studies are not always uniform, but on the whole, they suggest that functional connectivity between the hemispheres increases with age.

In this study, we examined the possibility that interhemispheric interaction works in much the same manner in the developing brain as it does in the adult brain. In particular, we believe that it provides a means to deal with increases in attentional demands and task complexity (for a review, see Banich, 1998). To vary computational complexity, we compare performance on two tasks. In general, our less complex task is a physical-identity task in which individuals decide if either of two probe items, one presented in each visual field, is physically identical to a laterally presented target item. The more complex task is generally a name-identity task. Here, individuals decide if either of two laterally presented uppercase probe letters has the same name as a laterally presented lowercase target item. The name-identity task is more computationally complex than the physical-identity task, because in addition to the demands of perceptual processing and decision making (as for the physical-identity task), one must also perform a case or name translation to determine if two letters match.

To investigate the effects of interhemispheric interaction, we compared performance on these tasks for two types of trials: within-hemisphere trials and across-hemisphere trials. On within-hemisphere trials, the target and matching probe are presented in the same visual field, and hence to the same hemisphere. Under such conditions, no interhemispheric interaction is necessary for a decision to be reached. In contrast, on across-hemisphere trials, the target and matching probe are presented in opposite visual fields. In this case, interhemispheric interaction must occur if the correct decision is to be reached.

We assume that the comparison of the two items depends mainly on the callosum, because split-brain patients are unable to produce correct match decisions when information is presented in opposite visual fields (e.g., Sergent, 1990; Sperry, Gazzaniga, & Bogen, 1969). Although recent work suggested that transfer of letters can be accomplished by acallosal individuals via the anterior commissure (Brown, Jeeves, Dietrich, & Burnison, 1999), we assumed that this channel plays a minor role in individuals who have an intact callosum, because it cannot support the transfer of such information under complex conditions.

In adults, we typically observe that across-hemisphere processing is more advantageous for computationally complex tasks than for less complex tasks (e.g., Banich & Belger, 1990; Banich, Stolar, Heller, & Goldman, 1992; Belger & Banich, 1992, 1998; Weissman & Banich, 1999). We interpreted these results as indicating an advantage to dividing processing across the hemispheres as task complexity increases. More specifically, when a task is computationally simple, it seems that the resources of one hemisphere are not overly taxed. In fact, the additional step of integrating information across the hemispheres actually appears to be detrimental to performance, because it adds a communication "overhead." In contrast, as tasks become more complex, the computational advantage afforded by dividing processing between the hemispheres more than offsets the additional cost of communication between them.

In this study, we examined whether a similar pattern would be observed in school-age children. Findings from a number of studies suggest that important developmental changes in interhemispheric integration occur between the ages of 9 and 11 years (e.g., Merola & Liederman, 1985), and hence our study centered on this age range.

There are a number of ways in which interhemispheric interaction may change as a function of computational complexity during development. One possibility is that there is little developmental change in this aspect of interhemispheric interaction. As reviewed elsewhere (Banich, 1998), we have argued that our results indicate a general processing advantage for dividing processing across the hemispheres when tasks are complex. In effect, we believe the effect is one of "mass action." The reasons for this conclusion are that the effect is observed across a variety of tasks (e.g., Banich & Passarotti, 2000; Weissman & Banich, 1999), response parameters (e.g., Banich & Passarotti, 2000), and modalities (e.g., Passarotti & Banich, 2000). Such an effect may not be influenced by the main developmental change in interhemispheric interaction, which is the decreased speed with which neural signals are transferred across the callosum. All that may matter would be whether a division of processing across the hemispheres is possible. Because children clearly are able to integrate information between the hemispheres (unlike split-brain patients), they may exhibit a pattern similar to adults.

Another possibility is that decreases in callosal transfer time with age may reduce the cost or overhead associated with interhemispheric communication. If this were the case, we would expect the relative advantage of across-hemisphere processing to increase with age. A final possibility is that interhemispheric processing may be more advantageous for younger than for older children. This result may be expected if one considers that interhemispheric interaction is especially useful under demanding conditions. Because younger children do not have the processing capacity of older children, they may rely more on across-hemisphere processing when dealing with increased processing demands. Such an effect would be most pronounced in the name-identity task, because it is computationally more complex.

Although this last prediction may seem counterintuitive, support for this possibility has been provided by work with older adults. There is much evidence that the cognitive processing capacity of older adults decreases with age (e.g., see Park & Schwarz, 2000). Recently, findings indicate that older adults exhibit a greater across-hemisphere advantage at lower levels of complexity than do younger adults (Reuter-Lorenz & Stanczak, this issue; Reuter-Lorenz, Stanczak, & Miller, 1999). Hence, older adults may rely on interhemispheric interaction as a compensatory mechanism to help deal with their diminished ability to cope with increased task complexity. A similar phenomenon may be observed in young children as well.

Another issue we wished to examine was whether there is a relation between certain aspects of attentional functioning and developmental aspects of interhemispheric interaction. Attention is a multifaceted entity encompassing many different processes including vigilance (sustained attention), selective attention with regard to spatial location or item attributes (e.g., color, form), response selection, and the management or allocation of resources required to successfully perform a task (e.g., LaBerge, 1990). As discussed previously, interaction between the hemispheres appears to modulate the information-processing capacity of the brain and as such can be considered an attentional function because it is a process that modulates the allocation of resources (for a review, see Banich, 1998).

The research examining a possible linkage between attentional functioning and developmental changes in interhemispheric interaction is relatively scant. However, one aspect of attention, sustained attention, has been linked to developmental changes in interchange between the hemispheres. Rueckert, Sorensen, and Levy (1994) showed that better performance on an interhemispheric matching task in children predicted better performance on a vigilance task. The interhemispheric task required individuals to compare lines on one, two, or three of the following dimensions: length, color, and orientation. In the within-hemisphere condition, the lines were presented to the same hemisphere, whereas in the across-hemisphere condition, the lines were presented to opposite hemispheres. In the vigilance task, individuals attended to a box and responded each time a briefly presented *X* appeared in the box. The authors found that children who were faster on across- than within-hemisphere processing were also generally faster on the vigilance task.

In a follow-up study, Rueckert and Levy (1996) found that better attentional performance was significantly correlated with less interhemispheric interference between motor programs. In particular, they examined the degree of interference that occurred when children were asked to draw a circle with one hand and a straight line with the other, as compared with the interference that occurred when drawing the same item with both hands. Children who exhibited higher levels of interference when drawing different items with each hand also exhibited deficits in sustained attention, especially at longer interstimulus intervals (i.e., 18 sec).

In this study, we wished to examine the relation between the degree to which interhemispheric processing helps the brain deal with computational complexity and another aspect of attention, selective attention for perceptual information. This exploration is motivated by our work with adults suggesting that selection of perceptual information can be modulated by interhemispheric interaction. For example, we have shown that interference between the local and global aspects of a hierarchically organized figure (e.g., a big *H* composed of little *S*s) can be reduced when the two items to be compared are initially directed to different hemispheres as opposed to being directed at a single hemisphere (Weissman & Banich, 1999). In this study, we were able to demonstrate that at least a portion of this modulation occurred at the level of perceptual selection. We found that interhemispheric interaction reduced interference more when the stimuli were composed of few local items, which made it harder perceptually to parse local and global information (Kimchi & Palmer, 1985), as compared to when the stimuli were composed of many local items, which allowed for an easier segregation.

Converging evidence for the role of interhemispheric interaction in the selection of perceptual information is provided by a study from our laboratory employing a lateralized version of the Stroop task in which a word is presented in one visual field and a color bar in the other. The individual's task is to name the color of a bar (e.g., red) while ignoring whether the word would facilitate (e.g., when the word is *red*) or interfere with such a response (e.g., when the word is *blue*). The closer the word is to the bar, the greater the interference provided by the word (e.g., Lowe & Mitterer, 1982). This finding suggests that a perceptual factor (i.e., the distance between the word and bar) influences how difficult it is to attentionally select the relevant information and block out conflicting information. In our study we had the word positioned either relatively close to the bar (2.9°) or further away (4.9°). We found that when the bar was closer to but not further from the word, the relative advantage of callosal transfer of information depended on attentional demands—whether the word's identity facilitated or interfered with performance. Because the effect of interhemispheric interaction varied with a perceptual factor, these results are consistent with Weissman and Banich (1999) in suggesting that interhemispheric interaction can modulate the selection of perceptual information.

If interaction between the hemispheres can modulate selective attention in adults, it would be of interest to know whether developmental changes in interhemispheric interaction would be associated with developmental changes in selective attention. To investigate this issue, we had children perform a free-vision version of a lateralized selective attention task that we have previously used with adults (Banich & Passarotti, 2000). This task requires selective attention, because the participants make a match decision based on the shape of items while ignoring their colors. Three items are presented on each trial, a target item and two probes. Participants decide if the target item matches one of the two probes in shape. To vary attentional demands, we manipulate the relation between the target and probes with regard to the attribute that is to be ignored (e.g., color). In conditions in which attentional demands are low, color information is congruent with form information (i.e., matching forms are the same color, mismatching forms are different colors). In contrast, in conditions in which attentional demands are high, color provides discordant information (i.e., matching forms are different colors, mismatching forms are the same color).

With adults, we found that the interfering effect of color could be modulated by interhemispheric interaction. That is, when matching items were presented in different visual fields as compared with the same visual field, the interfering effect of color was diminished. Hence, we have reason to believe that the ability to selectively attend to one item attribute over another (i.e., attend to form and not color) was aided by a division of processing between the hemispheres. Because performance on this task was modulated by interhemispheric interaction in adults, we reasoned that it was a good candidate task to employ with children.

In this study, we gave children a nonlateralized version of this task as a means of assessing selective attention without regard to within- or across-hemisphere processing. We then examined whether there was a relation between performance on this selective attention task and the tasks that we typically employ to examine interhemispheric interaction (i.e., the physical- and name-identity tasks). We reasoned that if interaction between the hemispheres helps increase the capacity for selective attention during development, we should observe a relation between the performances on the attentional and interhemispheric tasks.

METHOD

Participants

Twenty-four children between the ages of 6 and 14 years were recruited through school districts in the Champaign–Urbana area. Using a median split, the children were divided into two equal groups. The younger group included all children less than 10.5 years of age, and the older group included all children older than 10.5 years of age. All children were right-handed, had normal visual acuity, lacked a lateral phoria, and were not color-blind. Children with a history of learning disability were excluded from the sample.

Tasks

All children performed both the interhemispheric interaction and selective attention tasks.

Interhemispheric Task

Stimuli. Stimuli were the uppercase and lowercase versions of the letters *A, B, D, G, H, E, F, L, R, M, T,* and *Q* presented in Chicago font. Each display contained three black letters on a white background. Each letter subtended no more than 0.95° horizontally and 1.3° vertically. The two probe items were centered 1.6° above fixation and 2.68° laterally from midline, one in each visual field. The target item was centered 1.6° below fixation and 1.6° laterally from midline. For the physical-identity task, all items were uppercase letters. For the name-identity task, the two probes were presented in uppercase, and the target was presented in lowercase.

Half of all trials were match trials, in which one of the probes matched the target item, and half were mismatch trials, in which all three letters were different. For match trials, half were within-hemisphere trials, in which the target and the matching probe were presented in the same visual field, and half were across-hemisphere trials, in which the target and matching probe were presented in opposite visual fields. Within each of these conditions, the target was presented in the left visual field (LVF) for one half of the trials and in the right visual field (RVF) for the other half of the trials. Likewise for mismatch trials, the target appeared equally often in the LVF and RVF (see Figure 1).

Procedure. For each task, individuals received 20 practice trials and 120 test trials, which were divided into three blocks of 40 trials. The physical-identity task always preceded the name-identity task. At the beginning of a trial, a black square appeared for 300 msec; the abrupt onset of the square served to draw attention to this fixation point. Next, the three letters (along with a smaller fixation square) were displayed for 200 msec. After the stimulus display occurred, a blank white screen was displayed for 3,000 msec, during which time children were asked to press the space bar if there was a match and to refrain from responding if there was no match (go–no-go responses). Reaction time (RT) was recorded for each matching trial. This task required approximately 45 min for completion.

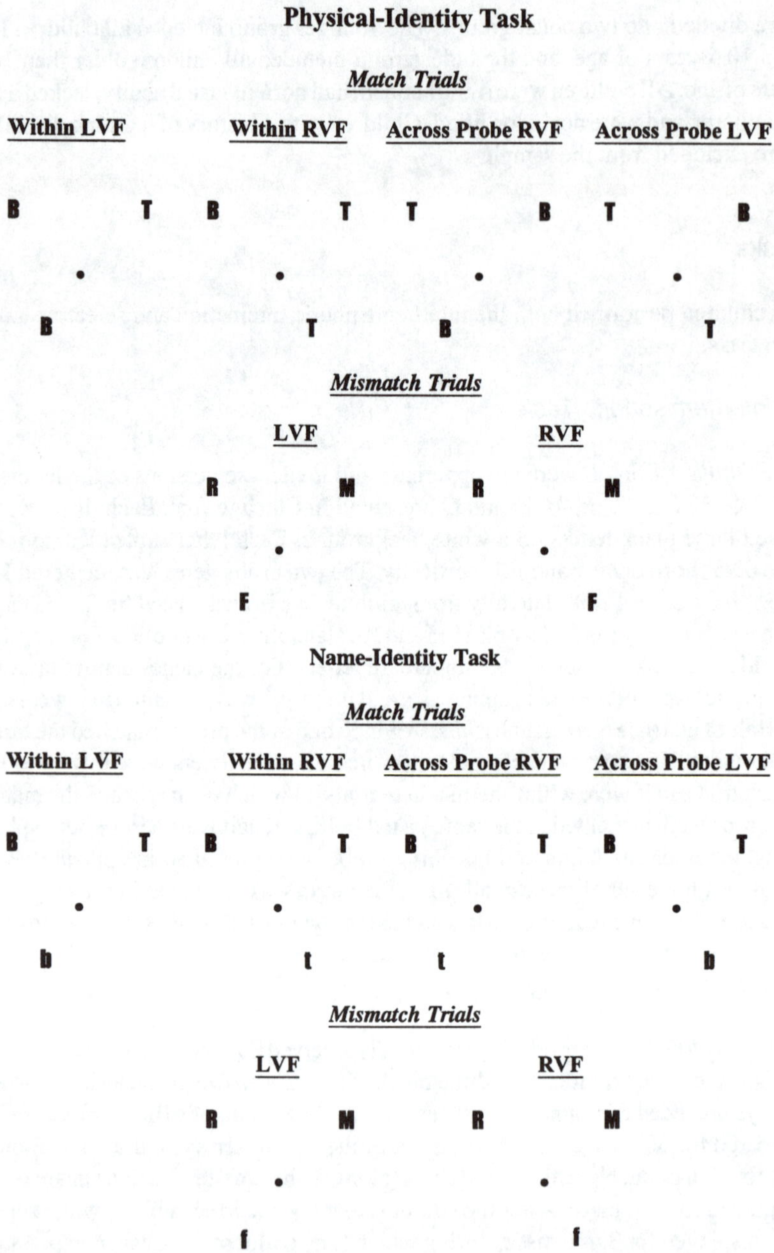

FIGURE 1 Sample match and mismatch trials for the interhemispheric task. *Note.* LVF = left visual field; RVF = right visual field.

Selective Attention Task

Stimuli. The stimulus array consisted of three geometric shapes arranged in the configuration of an inverted scalene triangle. We employed 16 colored shapes, which were created with the graphic software Adobe Photoshop 2.0.1. We used four exemplars of each of four shape categories: rectangles, ovals, triangles, and diamonds. All shapes covered an area of 0.25 cm^2 so that surface area would not provide a way to distinguish between them. The shapes subtended a maximum of 0.70° horizontally and 1.7° vertically. All shapes were colored, with four gradations for each of four color categories: green, brown, purple, and blue.

In our experimental array, the two probe items were always different shapes from each other. They were equally distant from the fixation point (2.8° lateral) and equally above it (1.4°). The bottom target item appeared at the same distance from the fixation cross (1.4°) as the top probe items, but laterally it was closer to fixation (1.4°) than the top probe items were. On half of the trials (match trials), the target shape was identical to one of the two probe shapes (e.g., both were equilateral triangles), and on one half of the trials (mismatch trials), the target was identical to neither shape. The bottom target was presented on the left for one half of the trials and on the right for the other half. Mismatch trials were constructed so that in one half of trials, all the items were different, but the target and one of the probes belonged to the same form category (e.g., an equilateral and an isosceles triangle). In the remaining half, each item was from a different form category.

To study selective attention, we varied the degree to which color facilitated or interfered with making the physical-identity decision. On one half of the match trials, the target and the same-form probe were identical in color (e.g., both midnight blue), and on one half they were from different color categories (e.g., midnight blue and lime green). Within each of these categories, trials were further divided so that on one half of the trials the different-form probe was identical in color to the target item (e.g., both were lime green), and on one half it was from a different color category. This arrangement provided for four different types of match trials, which can be considered to vary along a continuum in terms of the degree of selective attention required (see Figure 2).

In the first category of trials, the least selective attention was required, because the same-form probe matched the target in color (facilitating the decision that the probe matched the target) and because the different-form probe mismatched the target in color (helping to identify that probe as not matching the target). These trials were 16.7% of all match trials. In the second and third category of trials, an intermediate degree of selective attention was required. In the second category of trials, the same-form probe was different in color from the target (hindering recognition of the match in form), and the different-form probe was also distinct in color from the target (helping to identify that probe as not matching the target). These trials made up 33.3% of all match trials. In the third category, the same-form probe

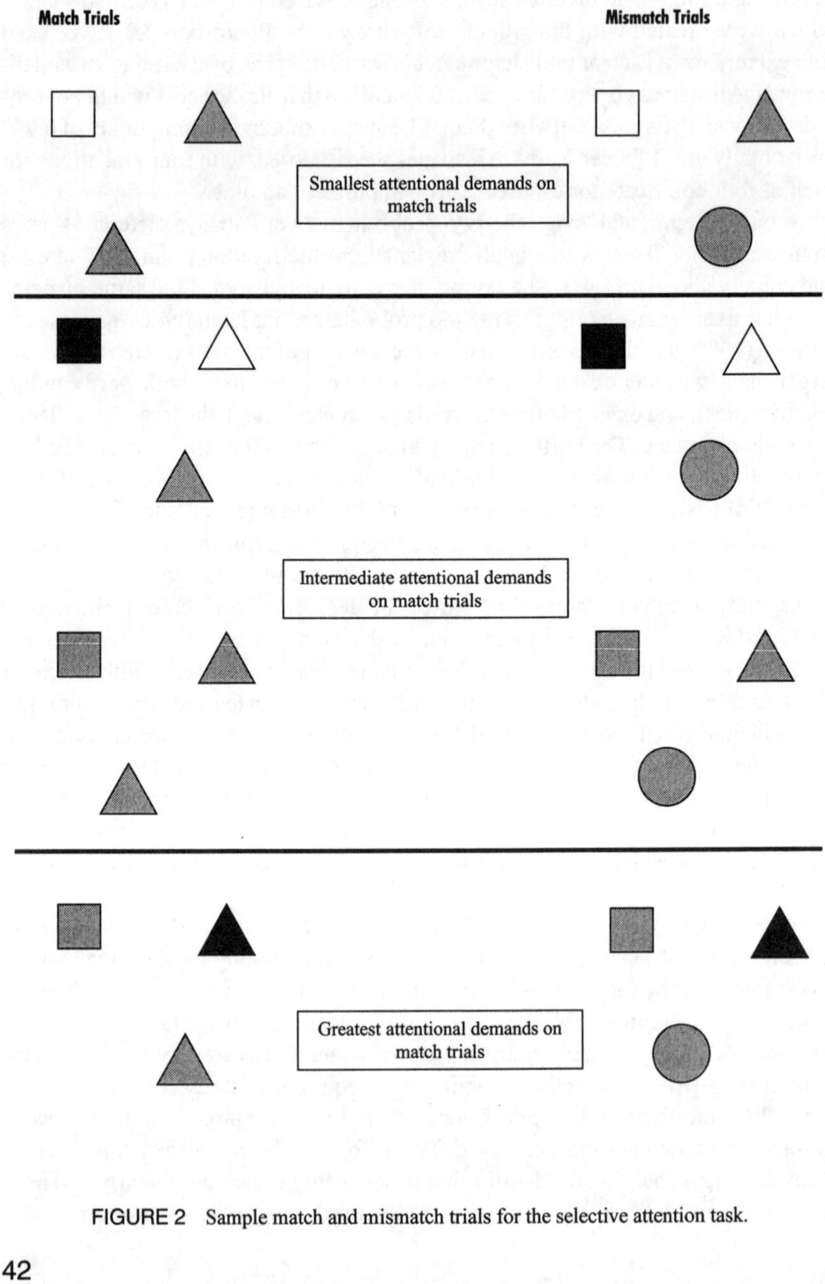

FIGURE 2 Sample match and mismatch trials for the selective attention task.

matched the target in color (facilitating the decision that the probe matched the target), and the different-form probe also matched the target in color (hindering the ability to identify that probe as not matching the target). These trials made up 33.3% of all match trials. The fourth category required the largest degree of selective attention. In this category, the same-form probe was different in color than the target (hindering the recognition of the match in form), and the different-form probe matched the target in color (hindering the ability to identify that probe as not matching the target). These trials were 16.7% of all match trials. When items were different colors, they were always from a different color category (e.g. green, blue, purple) and were never variants within a category (e.g., sky blue, azure).

Mismatch trials were similarly constructed with regard to variations in color (see Figure 2). In sum, the proportion of both match and mismatch trials were such that 33.3% of all trials were composed of items that were all the same color (e.g., all midnight blue), 33.3% were composed of trials in which two items were the same color and the third item was a different color (e.g., two midnight blue and one cherry red), and 33.3% were composed of trials in which all three items were different colors (e.g., one midnight blue, one cherry red, and one lime green).

Procedure. Children received 24 practice trials and 144 test trials that were equally divided across six blocks (two blocks of trials in which all the items were the same color, two blocks of trials in which two items were the same color and the third was a different color, and two blocks of trials in which each item was a unique color). On each trial the stimulus display appeared for 3,000 msec. Children indicated their decision by pressing the space bar if one of the probes was the same shape as the target and pressed no key if all shapes were different (go–no-go response). The hand used to respond was counterbalanced across blocks. This task required approximately 30 min for completion.

Equipment

Both tasks were presented on a Macintosh IIci computer with an Apple Color monitor. SuperLab software 1.55 was used to program the experiment. Children were seated in a comfortable chair 23.9 in. from the computer monitor with their heads in a chinrest to restrict head movements. They were provided with as many breaks as needed during the 1.25-hr test session.

RESULTS

Interhemispheric Task

RT. We performed repeated measures analysis of variance (ANOVA) on median RTs for match trials with *group* as the between-subject factor (younger = less than 10.5 years old; older = more than 10.5 years old). The within-subjects factors were *task* (physical identity, name identity), *trial type* (within hemisphere, across hemisphere), and *visual field of the matching probe* (LVF, RVF). We included this last factor in our analysis (visual field of the matching probe) because our prior work has suggested that the match decision is made by the hemisphere contralateral to this probe on both within-hemisphere and across-hemisphere trials (for a longer explanation, see Banich, 1995).

This analysis revealed a main effect of the group factor, $F(1, 22) = 4.48, p < .05$, reflecting the fact that younger children responded more slowly (631 msec) than older children did (506 msec). Because we did not wish our interpretation of the data to be confounded by this main effect, we transformed the data so that the across-hemisphere advantage was calculated as a percentage of mean RT [(average $RT_{\text{within hemisphere}}$ – average $RT_{\text{across hemisphere}}$)/overall average RT]. A negative value indicates a within-hemisphere advantage.

We then performed an ANOVA using the between-subject factors of group and the within-subjects factors of task and visual field of the matching probe. The only significant finding in this analysis was a main effect of task, $F(1, 22) = 13.14, p < .0025$. This reflected a significant 12.47% across-hemisphere advantage for the name-identity task, as compared with the insignificant –1.7% (i.e., within-hemisphere) advantage for the physical-identity task. Thus, like the pattern observed in adults, across-hemisphere communication is more advantageous in children as computational complexity increases. The Group × Task interaction did not reach conventional levels of significance, $F(1, 22) = 2.91, p = .10$, but results were in the direction of a larger across-hemisphere advantage for the younger children than for the older ones on the name-identity task (see Table 1). We obtained similar results when we used a normalized measure of performance (i.e., the difference in RT between within- and across-hemisphere trials divided by the standard deviation across all responses).

Accuracy. To obtain a measure of accuracy that was free from the response bias of individual children (e.g., responding impulsively or overly conservatively), we utilized d'. We performed repeated measures ANOVA on d', again using the same between- and within-subjects factors. This analysis revealed a main effect of task, $F(1, 22) = 8.19, p < .01$, and a significant Group × Task interaction, $F(1, 22) =$

TABLE 1
The Size of the Aross-Field Advantage as a Percentage of Mean Reaction Time

	Group	
Task	*Younger Children*	*Older Children*
Physical identity	–4.2%	0.0%
Name identity	16.8%	8.0%

7.61, $p < .03$. The younger children were significantly more accurate on the physical-identity task ($d' = 3.34$) than on the name-identity task ($d' = 2.52$), $F(1, 22) = 15.79$, $p < .001$, whereas there was no significant difference in accuracy between the two tasks for the older children (physical-identity task, $d' = 3.22$; name-identity task, $d' = 3.21$). Finally, there was a significant Task × Trial Type × Visual Field of the Matching Probe interaction, $F(1, 22) = 7.67$, $p < .03$. Decomposition of this interaction revealed that although there was a significant Task × Trial Type interaction for both visual fields, LVF: $F(1, 22) = 4.12$, $p < .05$; RVF: $F(1, 22) = 7.40$, $p < .03$, only the pattern for the RVF mimicked that observed previously in adults. When the matching probe was in the RVF, there was neither a within-hemisphere nor an across-hemisphere advantage for the physical-identity task, whereas a significant across-hemisphere advantage was observed for the name-identity task, $F(1, 22) = 4.30$, $p < .05$. In contrast, when the matching probe was in the LVF, there was an unexpected across-hemisphere advantage for the physical-identity task, $F(1, 22) = 5.44$, $p < .05$, and there was neither a within- nor an across-hemisphere advantage for the name-identity task. This pattern may reflect a speed–accuracy trade-off for LVF trials for the physical-identity task.

Selective Attention Task

RT. We performed a repeated measures ANOVA on median RT for match trials with the between-subject factor of group (younger, older) and the within-subjects factors of *color of same-form probe* (same as target, different than target) and *color of different-form probe* (same as target, different than target). This analysis revealed a main effect of color of same-form probe, $F(1, 22) = 56.26$, $p < .0001$, because, not surprisingly, responses were made significantly more quickly when the same-form probe was the same color as the target (993 msec) as compared with a different color (1,152 msec). There was also a significant Color of Same-Form Probe × Color of Different-Form Probe interaction, $F(1, 22) = 6.30$, $p < .025$, which was modified by a marginally significant interaction of Group × Color of Same-Form Probe × Color of Different-Form Probe, $F(1, 22) = 4.13$, $p < .06$. Tests on this three-way interaction indicated that it was entirely due to a Color of Same-Form Probe × Color of Different-Form Probe interaction for the younger group, $F(1, 22) = 10.32$, $p < .005$, because no effect existed for the older group ($p > .7$; see Table 2). For the younger group, when the target and same-form probe were the same color, responses were faster when the different-form probe was the same color as the target (985 msec) rather than a different color (1,065 msec). Hence, responses were speeded when all the stimuli were the same color as compared to when two of the stimuli were one color and the third stimulus was a different color. When the same-form probe and target were different colors, responses were faster when the different-form probe and target were different colors (i.e., when all three stimuli were different colors; 1,137 msec) rather than the same color (1,226 msec).

TABLE 2
Median Reaction Time in Milliseconds for the Selective Attention Task

	Different-Form Probe			
	Younger Children		*Older Children*	
Same-Form Probe	*Same Color*	*Different Color*	*Same Color*	*Different Color*
Same color	985	1,065	954	968
Different color	1,226	1,137	1,125	1,121

Once again, it appeared more difficult for the younger children to detect the matching probe when there was one distinctly colored stimulus.

Accuracy. An ANOVA on error rates (i.e., not detecting a match) was performed using the same between- and within-subjects factors as in the previous analysis. No significant results were obtained, although there was a trend for a main effect of Color of Same-Form Probe, $F(1, 22) = 3.41, p < .08$. This occurred because error rates tended to be lower when the matching probe was the same color as the target (1.2%) as compared to when the matching probe was a different color (3.7%).

Correlational Analyses

We performed a number of correlational analyses to examine the relations between age, interhemispheric interaction, and attention. To determine whether the degree of interhemispheric interaction changes as a function of age, for each task we correlated age and each dependent measure, d' and RT. The size of the across-hemisphere advantage for d' ($d'_{\text{across}} - d'_{\text{within}}$) and age were not correlated for either task. In contrast, the correlations between age and across-hemisphere advantage for RT were significant. For the physical-identity task, there was a significant positive correlation indicating that a younger age was associated with a larger within-hemisphere advantage, $r(22) = .40, p < .05$ (see Figure 3). In contrast, for the name-identity task, there was a significant negative correlation indicating that a younger age was associated with a larger across-hemisphere advantage, $r(22) = -.52, p < .01$ (see Figure 4). Hence, it appears from both these correlational analyses and the results of the ANOVA that younger age is associated with a greater differentiation between within- and across-hemisphere processing for the two tasks.

We examined the relation between age and attentional performance by correlating age with a measure of how much color interfered with making the decision based on form. Remember that in our trials the same-form probe (i.e., matching probe) could be either the same color as the target or different. We examined the correlations separately for each of these trial types. To obtain a measure of how

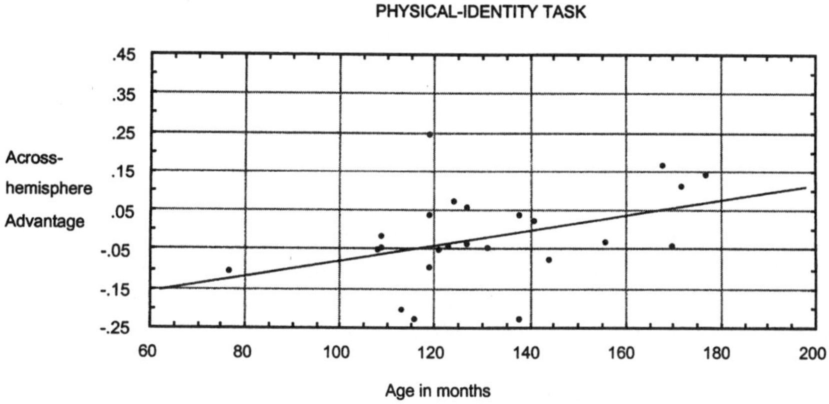

FIGURE 3 Correlation of age with the across-hemisphere advantage as a function of mean reaction time for the physical-identity task, $r(22) = .40, p < .05$. A negative value indicates a within-hemisphere advantage.

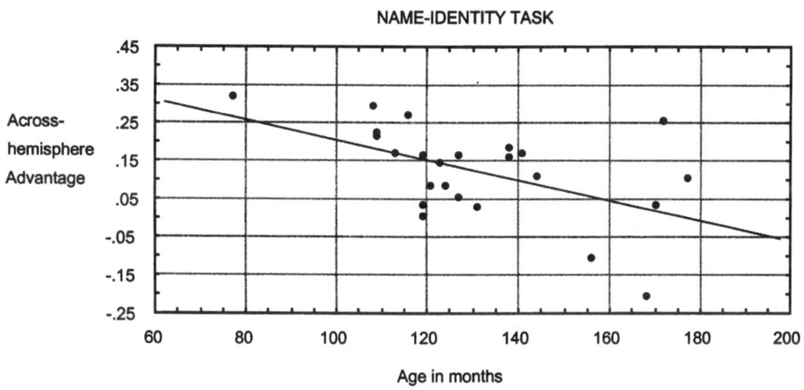

FIGURE 4 Correlation of age with the across-hemisphere advantage as a function of mean reaction time for the name-identity task, $r(22) = -.52, p < .01$. A negative value indicates a within-hemisphere advantage.

much color caused interference, we calculated how much longer it took an individual to respond when the different-form probe was the same color as the target (and hence would be distracting) as compared to when it was the same color.

When the same-form probe was the same color as the target, there was no correlation between age and the amount of interference engendered by the color of the different-form probe. However, when the same-form probe was a different color than the target, the correlation was significant, $r(22) = -.53, p < .01$. This correlation indicates that the younger the child, the more he or she was slowed in the detection of the matching form when the mismatching probe was the same color as the target, as compared with a different color. This correlation appears to indicate that when there is competing information (i.e., matching form but mismatching color), younger children are slower to ignore the task-irrelevant attribute (i.e., color).

Finally, we examined the correlation between the across-hemisphere advantage (as a percentage of RT) for each task and the ability to selectively attend. As our measure of selective attention, we utilized the degree to which RT was slowed (i.e., the degree to which a child was distracted) when the color of the different-form probe was the same color as the target, as compared to when it was different. There were no significant correlations for the physical-identity task. For the name-identity task, however, we found a positive correlation, $r(22) = .42, p < .05$, for trials on which the same-form probe was a different color than the target. For these trials, we found that a larger across-hemisphere advantage on the name-identity task was associated with a greater degree of interference from the different-form probe. Hence, those children who had the most difficulty in selective attention had the largest across-hemisphere advantage. This may seem to suggest that children who invoke across-hemisphere processing on the name-identity task are those who are less adept at attentional functioning. Such a finding would seem to be at odds with the idea that interaction between the hemispheres aids in reducing the effect of distracting information. This effect, however, seems to be mediated mainly by age, because the partial correlation between the across-hemisphere advantage and the interference by color after partialing out the effect of age was only .20.

DISCUSSION

The results of this experiment indicate that the relation between interhemispheric interaction and computational complexity in children is similar to that which we have previously observed in adults. As in adults, children appear to benefit from dividing processing across the hemispheres as computational complexity increases. This effect was reflected in the significant across-hemisphere advantage in RT for the more complex name-identity task and in the fact that there was neither a within- nor across-hemisphere advantage for the physical-identity task. This pattern was observed in both the younger group of children, aged 6 to 10.5 years, and the older group of children, aged 10.5 to 14 years. The accuracy data were only partially consistent, exhibiting a similar pattern (i.e., a greater across-hemisphere advantage for the name-identity than for the physical-identity task) for trials in which the matching probe was presented to the RVF but not the LVF. The reason for this discrepancy is not entirely clear. Overall, however, it appears that interaction between the hemispheres is moderated by computational complexity by the time children reach grammar school.

Nonetheless, the correlational analysis provided evidence for some changes in interhemispheric processing between the ages of 6 and 14. We found that the younger the child, the larger the within-hemisphere advantage on the physical-identity task and the larger the across-hemisphere advantage on the name-identity task. These results suggest that, if anything, the pattern we observe in adults is exaggerated in younger children. It appears unlikely that this pattern reflects the functioning of an immature callosum when one considers that the younger the children, the larger the across-hemisphere advantage. If the callosum of younger children were less functional, we would have expected a diminution in the size of the across-hemisphere advantage. Rather, we take these results to be consistent with our hypothesis that across-hemisphere processing is more advantageous under computationally complex conditions. Because younger children are more likely to be taxed by the demands of the name-identity task than older children, across-hemisphere processing becomes particularly advantageous. In this respect, the data from this study converge with those of Reuter-Lorenz et al. (1999) and of Reuter-Lorenz and Stanczak (this issue), who found a greater across-hemisphere advantage at lower levels of computational complexity in older than younger adults. Hence, populations particularly challenged by computational complexity may invoke across-hemisphere processing as a mechanism to cope with increased computational demands.

With regard to selective attention, we obtained evidence from both the ANOVA and the correlational analyses that older children were better able to ignore the distracting information provided by color when a decision was to be based on a stimulus's form. Such a result is not particularly surprising. However, it does verify the validity of our measure of selective attention as sensitive to developmental changes. More specifically, both groups of children were faster to detect the match in form when the target and same-form probe were the same color, as compared with different colors. The older children, however, were less influenced by the color of the different-form probe. Hence, the older children were more able to ignore color information that falsely suggested that the items matched when in fact their forms were different.

Despite finding evidence for developmental changes in the nature of interhemispheric interaction as a function of task complexity and the ability to selectively attend, we did not obtain strong evidence that these two processes covaried. Rather, the relation between these two variables appeared to be mediated by joint correlations with age. The lack of a relation in our data, however, does not preclude its existence, because such a relation could have been swamped by the effects of age. It is possible that the utility of interhemispheric interaction as a function of task complexity may predict individual differences in selective attention within a group of children who are all of more similar age. This issue must await future investigation.

In sum, our data indicate that by the grammar school years, interaction between the cerebral hemispheres acts a means to deal with computational complexity, as has previously been observed in adults. However, our correlation data provide evidence that the effects of interhemispheric interaction may not be entirely static during this time. Rather, it appeared that the younger the child, the more likely it is that interhemispheric interaction is beneficial to task performance. We suspect that this association occurs because younger children have less capacity within a single hemisphere to deal with computational complexity, making interaction more beneficial to performance. The implication of this finding, such as whether it influences the developmental course of mental functions such as attention, remains an open issue.

ACKNOWLEDGMENTS

Portions of this research project were supported by Grant R01 MH 54217 from the National Institute of Mental Health to Marie T. Banich.

We thank Laura Glaser for help in testing the children. We also thank Desiree White and Warren S. Brown for helpful comments on the article.

REFERENCES

Banich, M. T. (1995). Interhemispheric interaction: Mechanisms of unified processing. In F. L. Kitterle (Ed.), *Hemispheric communication: Mechanisms and models* (pp. 271–300). Hillsdale, NJ: Lawrence Erlbaum Associates, Inc.

Banich, M. T. (1998). The missing link: The role of interhemispheric interaction in attentional processing. *Brain and Cognition, 36,* 128–157.

Banich, M. T., & Belger, A. (1990). Interhemispheric interaction: How do the hemispheres divide and conquer a task? *Cortex, 26,* 77–94.

Banich, M. T., & Passarotti, A. (2000). *Interhemispheric interaction aids task performance under conditions of selective attention.* Manuscript submitted for publication.

Banich, M. T., Stolar, N., Heller, W., & Goldman, R. (1992). A deficit in right-hemisphere performance after induction of a depressed mood. *Neuropsychiatry, Neuropsychology, and Behavioral Neurology, 5,* 20–27.

Belger, A., & Banich, M. T. (1992). Interhemispheric interaction affected by computational complexity. *Neuropsychologia, 30,* 923–931.

Belger, A., & Banich, M. T. (1998). Costs and benefits of integrating information between the cerebral hemispheres: A computational perspective. *Neuropsychology, 12,* 380–398.

Brizzolara, D., Ferretti, G., Brovedani, P., Casalini, C., & Sbrana, B. (1994). Is interhemispheric transfer time related to age? A developmental study. *Behavioral Brain Research, 64,* 179–184.

Brown, W. S., Jeeves, M. A., Dietrich, R., & Burnison, D. S. (1999). Bilateral field advantage and evoked potential interhemispheric transmission in commissurotomy and callosal agenesis. *Neuropsychologia, 37,* 1165–1180.

Giedd, J. N., Rumsey, J. M., Castellanos, F. X., Rajapakse, J. C., Kaysen, D., Vaituzis, A. C., Vauss, Y. C., Hamburger, S. D., & Rapoport, J. L. (1996). A quantitative MRI study of the corpus callosum in children and adolescents. *Developmental Brain Research, 91,* 274–280.

Hagelthorn, K. M., Brown, W. S., Amano S., & Asarnow, R. (2000/this issue). Normal development of bilateral field advantage and evoked potential interhemispheric transmission time. *Developmental Neuropsychology, 18,* 11–31.

Kimchi, R., & Palmer, S. E. (1985). Separability and integrality of global and local levels of hierarchical patterns. *Journal of Experimental Psychology: Human Perception and Performance, 11,* 673–688.

LaBerge, D. L. (1990). Attention. *Psychological Science, 1,* 156–162.

Liederman, J., Merola, J., & Hoffman, C. (1986). Longitudinal data indicate that hemispheric independence increases during early adolescence. *Developmental Neuropsychology, 2,* 183–201.

Lowe, D. G., & Mitterer, J. O. (1982). Selective and divided attention in a Stroop task. *Canadian Journal of Psychology, 36,* 684–700.

Merola, J., & Liederman, J. (1985). Developmental changes in hemispheric independence. *Child Development, 56,* 1184–1194.

O'Leary, D. S. (1980). A developmental study of interhemispheric transfer in children aged five to ten. *Child Development, 51,* 743–750.

Park, D., & Schwarz, N. (Eds.). (2000). *Cognitive aging: A primer.* Philadelphia: Psychology Press.

Passarotti, A., & Banich, M. T. (2000). *A generalized role of interhemispheric interaction under attentionally-demanding conditions: Evidence from the auditory and tactile modalities.* Manuscript submitted for publication.

Quinn, K., & Geffen, G. (1986). The development of tactile transfer of information. *Neuropsychologia, 24,* 793–804.

Ratinckx, E., Brysbaert, M., & d'Ydewalle, G. (1997). Age and interhemispheric transfer time: A failure to replicate. *Behavioural Brain Research, 86,* 161–164.

Reuter-Lorenz, P. A., & Stanczak, L. (2000/this issue). Differential effects of aging on the functions of the corpus callosum. *Developmental Neuropsychology, 18,* 113–137.

Reuter-Lorenz, P. A., Stanczak, L., & Miller, A. (1999). Neural recruitment and cognitive aging: Two hemispheres are better than one, especially as you age. *Psychological Science, 10,* 494–500.

Rueckert, L., & Levy, J. (1996). Further evidence that the callosum is involved in sustaining attention. *Neuropsychologia, 34,* 927–935.

Rueckert, L., Sorensen, L., & Levy, J. (1994). Callosal efficiency is related to sustained attention. *Neuropsychologia, 32,* 159–173.

Salamy, A. (1978). Commissural transmission: Maturational changes in humans. *Science, 22,* 1409–1411.

Sergent, J. (1990). Furtive incursions into bicameral minds: Integrating and coordinating role of subcortical structures. *Brain, 113,* 537–568.

Sperry, R. W., Gazzaniga, M. S., & Bogen, J. E. (1969). Interhemispheric relationships: The neocortical commissures: Syndromes of hemisphere disconnection. In P. J. Vinken & G. W. Bruyn (Eds.), *Handbook of clinical neurology* (pp. 273–290). Amsterdam: Elsevier.

Weissman, D. H., & Banich, M. T. (1999). A role for interhemispheric communication in reducing the effects of global–local interference. *Journal of Experimental Psychology: General, 128,* 283–308.

DEVELOPMENTAL NEUROPSYCHOLOGY, *18*(1), 53–71

Interhemispheric Interaction During Childhood: II. Children With Early-Treated Phenylketonuria

Marie T. Banich
The Beckman Institute
Department of Psychology
University of Illinois at Urbana–Champaign

Alessandra M. Passarotti
Department of Cognitive Sciences
University of California at San Diego

Desirée A. White and Marsha J. Nortz
Department of Psychology
Washington University

Robert D. Steiner
Departments of Pediatrics and Molecular Genetics,
Child Development and Rehabilitation Center,
Doernbecher Children's Hospital,
Oregon Health Sciences University, Portland

This study examined whether children with early-treated phenylketonuria (ETPKU) exhibited a disruption in communication between the hemispheres as a function of computational complexity (Banich & Belger, 1990; Belger & Banich, 1992, 1998) when compared to neurologically uncompromised children who were matched in age and IQ. This investigation was motivated by findings that phenylketonuria affects myelination of neurons, including those that make up the corpus callosum, the main neural conduit for interhemispheric interaction. Children performed 2 tasks: a less

Requests for reprints should be sent to Marie T. Banich, Department of Psychology, University of Colorado at Boulder, UCB 345, Boulder, CO 80309. E-mail: mbanich@psych.colorado.edu

complex physical-identity task and a more complex name-identity task. For both tasks, we compared performance on across-hemisphere trials, which require interhemispheric interaction, and on within-hemisphere trials, in which no hemispheric interaction is required. On the more complex name-identity task, children with ETPKU exhibited less of a benefit from across-hemisphere processing than did neurologically intact children. These results suggest that the interhemispheric interaction required to complete computationally complex tasks is compromised in children with ETPKU. Such an insufficiency may explain some of the attentional deficits observed in this group of children.

In this study, we examined interactions between the cerebral hemispheres in a group of children with early-treated phenylketonuria (ETPKU) as compared to children without neurological compromise. Phenylketonuria (PKU) has been demonstrated to affect myelination of neurons in both humans (e.g., Bauman & Kemper, 1982; Macombe et al., 1992) and animals (Reynolds, Burri, Mahal, & Herschkowitz, 1992). The corpus callosum, a massive white matter tract connecting the cerebral hemispheres, becomes heavily myelinated during childhood (Giedd et al., 1996; Yakovlev & Lecours, 1967). Hence, PKU may be expected to affect interhemispheric interaction.

PKU is a genetic disorder that produces an inborn error of metabolism caused by a deficiency of the enzyme phenylalanine hydroxylase (Woo, Lidsky, Güttler, Chandra, & Robson, 1983). The result is that phenylalanine (an amino acid) is not efficiently converted into tyrosine (another amino acid), which is a precursor of dopamine (a neurotransmitter). High levels of phenylalanine can lead to mental retardation (Koch, Azen, Friedman, & Williamson, 1982). Furthermore, glial cells are especially vulnerable in PKU, resulting in the noted compromise of myelination (Dyer et al., 1996).

Because of the negative effects of PKU, many countries have implemented mandatory screening for PKU at birth (e.g., Lund & Wamberg, 1970; Starfield & Holtzman, 1975). Neonates who screen positive are placed on a diet to restrict the intake of phenylalanine (Bickel, Gerrard, & Hicksman, 1954; Hudson, Mordaunt, & Leahy, 1970). Nonetheless, children with ETPKU may experience subtle deficits in cognition. For example, an overall drop in IQ relative to siblings has been observed (Dobson, Kushida, Williamson, & Friedman, 1976) and appears to be more pronounced when dietary control is poor (e.g., Smith, Beasley, & Ades, 1991). Although disruptions in myelination can be partially ameliorated through dietary control (e.g., Thompson et al., 1993), other evidence points to persisting white matter abnormalities (e.g., Bick et al., 1991).

The association between PKU and disrupted myelination led Gourovitch, Craft, Dowton, Ambrose, and Sparta (1994) to examine interhemispheric interaction in individuals with ETPKU who ranged from 6 to 23 years of age. These researchers used the standard Poffenberger (1912) paradigm to examine the crossed–uncrossed difference (CUD) as an estimate of interhemispheric transfer time. In this paradigm, individuals must respond to a simple laterally presented visual stimulus (e.g., a light flash) by depressing a response key. In the uncrossed condition, the responding hand is controlled by the same hemisphere as that which receives the stimulus (e.g., a right-hand response is given to a stimulus presented to the right visual field [RVF]). In the crossed condition, the responding hand is controlled by the opposite hemisphere (e.g., RVF stimulus and left-hand response). In this case, information must cross the corpus callosum before a response can be initiated. The elongation of reaction time (RT) on the crossed condition relative to the uncrossed condition is taken as a measure of interhemispheric transfer time.

Gourovitch et al. (1994) found that individuals with ETPKU exhibited an exaggerated slowing in RT when the left hand was used to respond to targets presented in the RVF. They interpreted these results as indicating that interhemispheric transfer from the left to the right hemisphere was compromised in individuals with ETPKU as compared with their two other study groups (neurologically intact children and children with attention deficit hyperactivity disorder). In addition, the results revealed that a greater degree of slowing of interhemispheric transfer from the left hemisphere to the right was associated with higher phenylalanine levels at birth.

In addition to compromising the process of myelination, PKU also appears to selectively affect regions of the brain that are highly innervated by dopaminergic neurons. Studies have shown that phenylalanine levels are negatively correlated with dopamine level in individuals with PKU (e.g., Krause et al., 1985). Children with PKU exhibit deficits in contrast sensitivity, which has been suggested to be caused by abnormal functioning of retinal neurons, whose functioning is highly dependent on dopamine (Diamond & Herzberg, 1996). In addition, there are numerous reports that children with ETPKU experience dysfunction in a variety of cognitive abilities subserved by the frontal lobes (e.g., Diamond, Prevor, Callender, & Druin, 1997), a brain region that receives substantial dopaminergic innervation. For example, Smith, Klim, Mallozzi, and Hanley (1996) found that children with ETPKU showed greater deficits on tasks subserved by frontal as compared to posterior regions of the brain, and that the degree of phenylalanine elevation was significantly correlated with performance on tasks tapping frontal but not posterior brain function. Deficits on attentional tasks subserved by the frontal lobes (e.g., the Stroop task) were also revealed, and again, performance on these tasks was significantly correlated with serum phenylalanine levels (e.g., Weglage, Pietsch, Funders, Koch, & Ullrich, 1996).

It has been suggested that dopaminergic innervation is especially important for left-hemisphere function (e.g., Tucker & Williamson, 1984), which raises the possibility that children with PKU may exhibit specific left-hemisphere dysfunction. Such an association is suggested by the work of Craft, Gourovitch, Dowton,

Swanson, and Bonforte (1992). They used the Posner attention-cueing paradigm and found that males with ETPKU exhibited slowed responses to RVF targets following a left visual field (LVF) cue. This pattern is similar to that observed in patients with damage to the left parietal lobe and has been interpreted as a left-hemisphere deficit in the ability to disengage attention. In this situation, attention is first engaged by the LVF cue. Then attention must be disengaged before it can be moved in a rightward direction to the RVF target. The left hemisphere would be responsible for disengaging attention so that it could be moved in a rightward direction. In contrast, the right hemisphere would be responsible for disengaging attention such that it could be moved in a leftward direction (e.g., Kinsbourne, 1993; Posner, Inhoff, Friedrich, & Cohen, 1987). These authors suggested that such left-hemisphere dysfunction was mediated by dopamine, as they found a correlation between the phenylalanine levels at the time of testing and the degree of the disengagement deficit for males (at least when the delay between the cue and target was 800 msec).

In this study we wished to address two issues. First, we wished to examine whether children with ETPKU would exhibit deficits in interhemispheric interaction for higher order information rather than for the simple visual light flashes used in the Gourovitch et al. (1994) study. To do so, we used two matching tasks, one in which children decided if letters were physically identical (physical-identity task) and one in which they decided if letters had the same name (name-identity task). We also chose these tasks because it has been shown previously that the utility of interhemispheric interaction varies as a function of computational complexity (e.g., Banich & Belger, 1990; Belger & Banich, 1992, 1998; Weissman & Banich, 1999). The name-identity task is more complex than the physical-identity task, because not only must items be encoded on the basis of their physical characteristics and a response emitted, but the letters must be transformed into some other code (e.g., a case-neutral code, a name code) before a decision can be made.

In brief, our prior studies have shown that when tasks are relatively simple, they are performed more rapidly and accurately by one hemisphere as compared with having both hemispheres cooperate to perform the task. In contrast, for more complex tasks, across-hemisphere processing provides a performance advantage. In our previous work, we have shown that these effects are observed in both adults (Banich & Belger, 1990; Belger & Banich, 1992, 1998) and school-age children (Banich, Passarotti, & Janes, this issue). We have suggested that a within-hemisphere advantage occurs under conditions of low complexity because there is no computational gain from dividing processing across the hemispheres to offset the costs entailed in the "overhead" of coordinating processing across the hemispheres. For more computationally complex tasks, however, this overhead is relatively less important compared to the computational power gained by dividing processing across the hemispheres; this results in the across-hemisphere advantage.

The issue explored in this study was whether children with ETPKU would exhibit a pattern of performance similar to that of neurologically intact children. To differentiate between various possible types of interhemispheric deficits, it was important that two tasks be used, one that yielded a within-hemisphere advantage and one that yielded an across-hemisphere advantage (for a more detailed discussion, see Banich & Shenker, 1994). One possibility is that ETPKU may impede interhemispheric interaction such that performance on all across-hemisphere trials is disrupted. In this case, children with ETPKU would exhibit performance more similar to that of patients with callosal dysfunction or callosal disconnection. On the other hand, the deficit could be more subtle and may emerge only when across-hemisphere processing is critical or beneficial to task performance, as under conditions of high complexity. In this case, we would expect to observe the deficit on the name-identity task but not on the physical-identity task.

The second issue we wished to further explore was the possibility that children with ETPKU exhibit a specific deficit in left-hemisphere function. The Banich and Belger (1990) paradigm is especially useful in this regard because it allows one to examine not only differences between within- and across-hemisphere processing, but hemispheric differences as well, both on within- and across-hemisphere trials. In our paradigm, three items are presented on every trial. A lateralized target item appears below two probes, one positioned in each visual field. On within-hemisphere trials, both matching items are presented in the same visual field, and hence we assume that the decision is subserved by the contralateral hemisphere (e.g., the left hemisphere makes the match decision when the matching items are presented in the RVF). On across-hemisphere trials, each hemisphere receives one of the matching items, which allows for the possibility that either hemisphere could make the match decision.

Our prior research has allowed us to determine which hemisphere makes the match decision on across-hemisphere trials. We have evidence that the decision is made by the hemisphere contralateral to the matching probe item. Hence, when the target is presented in the LVF and the probe is presented in the RVF (across-probe RVF trials), the decision is subserved by the left hemisphere. In contrast, when the target is presented in the RVF and the probe is presented in the LVF (across-probe LVF trials), the decision is subserved by the right hemisphere (see Figure 1).

Evidence for this assertion comes from a study in which we manipulated the mood of our participants into one of two mood states, either neutral or sad. Consistent with prior reports that a sad mood differentially affects right-hemisphere performance (e.g., Ladavas, Nicoletti, Umilta, & Rizzolatti, 1984), we found that, compared with a neutral mood state, a sad mood state reduced performance on within-hemisphere LVF trials relative to within-hemisphere RVF trials. Likewise, we found a reduction in performance on across-probe LVF trials relative to across-probe RVF trials, suggesting that the match decision is made by the right hemisphere on across-probe LVF trials (Banich, Stolar, Heller, & Goldman,

Physical-Identity Task

Match Trials

Within LVF	**Within RVF**	**Across Probe RVF**	**Across Probe LVF**
G F	G F	G F	G F
.	.	.	.
G	F	F	G

Mismatch Trials

LVF	**RVF**
M R	M R
.	.
Q	Q

Name-Identity Task

Match Trials

Within LVF	**Within RVF**	**Across Probe RVF**	**Across Probe LVF**
H L	H L	H L	H L
.	.	.	.
h	l	l	h

Mismatch Trials

LVF	**RVF**
T R	T R
.	.
d	d

FIGURE 1 Sample trials for the physical-identity and name-identity tasks. Note. LVF = left visual field; RVF = right visual field.

1992). Thus, if children with ETPKU have specific left-hemisphere dysfunction, their performance should be compromised on within-RVF trials and on across-probe RVF trials.

In sum, we had two main objectives in our study. First, we wished to determine if children with ETPKU exhibit a disruption in interhemispheric processing. If such a disruption were observed, we wished to more carefully characterize it, determining whether it was exhibited under all conditions or only under situations with high computational demands. Second, we wished to examine whether there is any evidence that either hemispheric or interhemispheric processing is asymmetrically disrupted in children with ETPKU. More specifically, we wished to examine whether children with ETPKU exhibited left-hemisphere dysfunction or disruption in the transfer of information from the left hemisphere to the right.

METHOD

Participants

Participants were 9 children with ETPKU and 12 neurologically intact children. Children with ETPKU were recruited through the Phenylketonuria Clinic in the Division of Medical Genetics/Department of Pediatrics at St. Louis Children's Hospital, Washington University School of Medicine. All of the children had been diagnosed with PKU prior to 6 weeks of age and were on a diet to restrict phenylalanine intake at the time of participation. The phenylalanine levels obtained closest to time of participation in our study ranged from 5.9 mg/dl to 13.7 mg/dl (M = 9.67 mg/dl, SD = 3.0 mg/dl). The neurologically intact children were from the St. Louis community.

None of the children in either the ETPKU or the neurologically intact groups had histories of learning disabilities or major medical disorders other than PKU. Children in the ETPKU group ranged from 6 to 15 years of age, whereas children in the neurologically intact group ranged from 7 to 14 years of age. Mean ages for the ETPKU and for the neurologically intact groups were 10.6 (SD = 2.8) and 10.7 (SD = 2.2) years, respectively. General intellectual abilities (i.e., IQ) as estimated by the Picture Vocabulary subtest from the Woodcock–Johnson Psychoeducational Battery–Revised (Woodcock & Johnson, 1989) ranged from 96 to 125 for the ETPKU group and from 90 to 138 for the neurologically intact group. Mean estimated IQs for the ETPKU and for the neurologically intact groups were 114 (SD = 11.9) and 116 (SD = 16.1), respectively. There were no significant between-group differences on any of these variables (see Table 1).

The sample of ETPKU children consisted of two right-handed boys, two left-handed boys, four right-handed girls, and one left-handed girl. The sample of neurologically intact children consisted of two right-handed boys, two

TABLE 1
Characteristics of Phenylketonuria and Neurologically Intact Participants

Group	Sex	Handedness	Age at Testing[a]	PPVT (Standardized)[b]
Phenylketonuria intact individuals				
1	Male	Right	12.25	124
2	Female	Right	7.50	110
3	Female	Right	9.00	122
4	Female	Left	9.25	120
5	Female	Right	6.75	125
6	Male	Right	13.75	100
7	Male	Left	11.00	124
8	Female	Right	15.00	96
9	Male	Left	10.75	101
Neurologically intact individuals				
1	Female	Right	11.00	115
2	Male	Right	12.75	94
3	Female	Left	12.50	90
4	Female	Right	8.75	128
5	Male	Left	13.75	118
6	Female	Right	9.75	104
7	Female	Right	14.00	135
8	Male	Right	11.50	120
9	Female	Right	9.00	132
10	Female	Right	8.75	138
11	Female	Right	7.75	112
12	Male	Left	8.50	100

Note. PPVT = Peabody Picture Vocabulary Test.

[a]For the phenylketonuria-intact group, mean age at testing was 10.58 years (SD = 2.76). For the neurologically-intact group, mean age was 10.67 years (SD = 2.20).

[b]For the phenylketonuria-intact group, mean PPVT was 113.56 (SD = 11.85). For the neurologically-intact group, mean PPVT was 115.50 (SD = 16.07).

left-handed boys, seven right-handed girls, and one left-handed girl. Previously, we have found no difference between right- and left-handed adults in the interhemispheric processing measures employed in this study (Belger & Banich, 1998).

Procedure

Children were administered the Banich and Belger (1990) interhemispheric task as part of a larger neuropsychological test battery. Results from this battery will be reported elsewhere. It should be noted that the procedure used in this study (and described later) was identical to that of Banich, Passarotti, and Janes (this issue), except that, because of time constraints, there were fewer experimental trials.

Stimuli. Stimuli were the uppercase and lowercase versions of the letters *A, B, D, E, F, G, H, L, M, Q, R,* and *T* presented in Chicago font. Each display contained three black letters on a white background. Each letter subtended no more than .95° horizontally and 1.3° vertically. The two probe items were centered 1.6° above fixation and 2.68° laterally from midline, with one in each visual field. The target item was centered 1.6° below fixation and 1.6° laterally from midline. For the physical-identity task, all items were uppercase letters. For the name-identity task, the two probes were presented in uppercase and the target was presented in lowercase.

One half of all trials were match trials, in which one of the probes matched the target item, and half were mismatch trials, in which all three letters were different. For match trials, half were within-hemisphere trials, in which the target and the matching probe were presented in the same visual field, and half were across-hemisphere trials, in which the target and matching probe were presented in opposite visual fields. For all conditions in both match and mismatch trials, the target appeared equally often in the LVF and RVF (see Figure 1).

Experimental presentation. Children received 8 practice trials and 80 test trials. At the beginning of a trial, a black square appeared for 300 msec, drawing attention to this fixation point. Next, the three letters (along with a smaller fixation square) were displayed for 200 msec. After the stimulus display, a blank white screen appeared for 3,000 msec, during which time children were asked to press the space bar if there were a match and to refrain from responding if there were no match (go–no-go responses). RT was recorded for each matching trial. The task required approximately 45 min to complete.

Equipment

The task was run on a Macintosh Plus with SuperLab 1.55 software.

RESULTS

Accuracy

To obtain a measure of accuracy that was free from the response biases of individual children (e.g., responding impulsively or overly conservatively), we utilized d'. We performed a repeated measures analysis of variance (ANOVA) on d' with the between-subject factor of *group* (ETPKU, neurologically intact) and the within-subjects factors of *task* (physical identity, name identity), *trial type* (within hemisphere, across hemisphere), and *visual field of the matching probe*

(LVF, RVF). We included this last factor (visual field of the matching probe) in our analysis because our prior work suggested that the match decision is made by the hemisphere contralateral to this probe on both within-hemisphere and across-hemisphere trials (see Banich, 1995, for a longer explanation).

The analysis revealed a main effect of task, $F(1, 18) = 23.54, p < .0003$, because accuracy was higher for the physical-identity task ($d' = 3.65$) than for the name-identity task ($d' = 2.96$). A main effect of trial type was also observed, $F(1, 18) = 8.74, p < .01$, as responses were more accurate on across-hemisphere trials ($d' = 3.41$) than on within-hemisphere trials ($d' = 3.20$). Both of these effects were modified by a significant four-way Group × Task × Trial Type × Visual Field of the Matching Probe interaction, $F(1, 18) = 9.98, p < .005$ (see Figures 2 and 3).

Decomposition of this interaction indicated that the Group × Trial Type × Visual Field of the Matching Probe interaction was not significant for the physical-identity task. On this task, neither group exhibited either a within- or an across-hemisphere advantage ($p > .10$). In contrast, the Group × Trial Type × Visual Field of the Matching Probe interaction was significant for the name-identity task, $F(1, 18) = 11.06, p < .005$. Decomposition of this interaction revealed that the patterns did not differ for the ETPKU and neurologically intact groups for LVF-probe name-identity trials because neither group exhibited a within- or an across-hemisphere advantage. However, the pattern for the two groups differed on

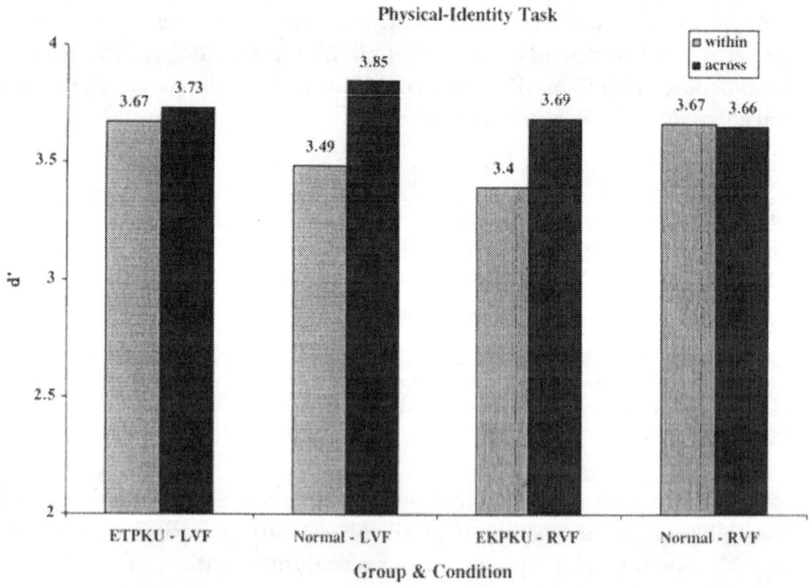

FIGURE 2 Mean accuracy (d') for the physical-identity task. *Note.* ETPKU = early-treated phenylketonuria; LVF = left visual field matching probe; RVF = right visual field matching probe.

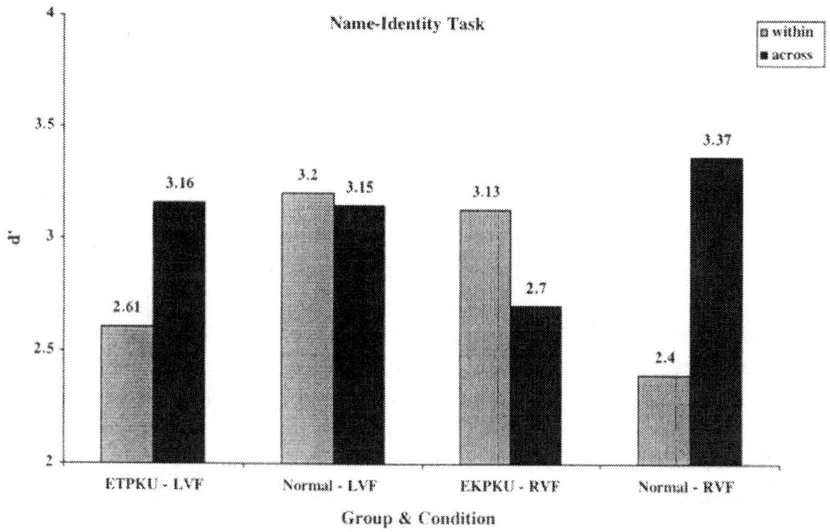

FIGURE 3 Mean accuracy (*d'*) for the name-identity task. *Note.* ETPKU = early-treated phenylketonuria; LVF = left visual field matching probe; RVF = right visual field matching probe.

RVF-probe name-identity trials, $F(1, 18) = 18.16$, $p < .0005$. The ETPKU group exhibited neither a within- nor an across-hemisphere advantage ($p > .09$), whereas the neurologically intact group exhibited a highly significant across-hemisphere advantage, $F(1, 18) = 19.42$, $p < .0005$, a pattern also observed in a separate sample of neurologically intact children (Banich, Passarotti, & Janes, this issue).

To examine whether there was any evidence of a specific left-hemisphere deficit in children with ETPKU, we performed tests of simple effects to compare their responses on RVF-probe name-identity trials to those of the neurologically intact group. There were no significant differences in performance between the groups for either within-hemisphere or across-hemisphere trials.

RT

We performed a repeated measures ANOVA on median RT using the same between- and within-subjects factors as noted previously. As in the d' analysis, this analysis revealed a main effect of Task, $F(1, 18) = 80.73$, $p < .0001$, as RT for physical-identity trials (520 msec) was faster than that for name-identity trials (728 msec). A main effect of trial type was also observed, $F(1, 18) = 5.55$, $p < .05$, as RT for within-hemisphere trials (605 msec) was faster than that for across-hemisphere trials (643 msec). The main effect of trial type was opposite to that found for d'. Because there were several higher order significant interactions that modified this main effect, we discuss the possibility of a speed–accuracy trade-off when we consider these higher order effects. These included significant interactions of Trial Type × Visual Field of the Matching Probe, $F(1, 18) = 8.09, p < .03$, and of Task × Trial Type × Visual Field of the Matching Probe, $F(1, 18) = 9.60, p < .01$.

Although the four-way interaction of Group × Task × Trial Type × Visual Field of the Matching Probe did not reach conventional levels of significance ($p < .20$), we performed a decomposition similar to that performed on the d' data to look for correspondence between the two measures of performance (i.e., d' and median RT.

As with the d' data, there was no Group × Trial Type × Visual Field of the Matching Probe interaction for the physical-identity task ($p > .40$) because both groups demonstrated a significant within-hemisphere advantage, $F(1, 18) = 14.38, p < .003$. For the name-identity task, the Group × Trial Type × Visual Field of the Matching Probe interaction approached significance ($p < .10$). Similar to the d' data, there was no group difference in the processing of LVF-probe trials for the name-identity task ($p > .35$). Surprisingly, both groups showed a significant within-hemisphere advantage, $F(1, 18) = 5.89, p < .05$. Although we may have expected a within-hemisphere advantage for the ETPKU group, we would not have expected such a pattern for the neurologically intact children. Previous results with

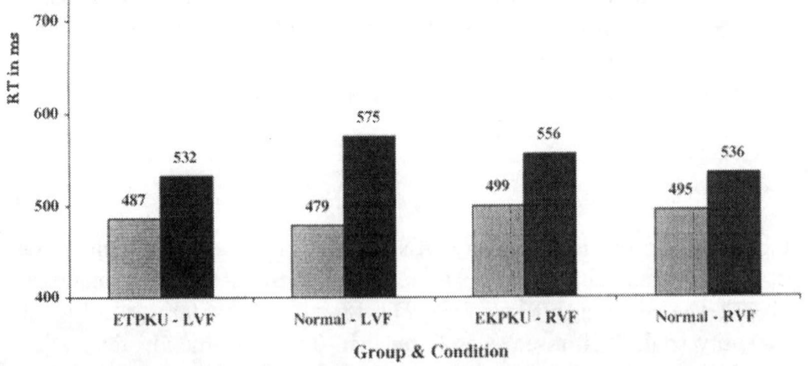

FIGURE 4 Median reaction time (RT) for the physical-identity task. *Note.* ETPKU = early-treated phenylketonuria; LVF = left visual field matching probe; RVF = right visual field matching probe.

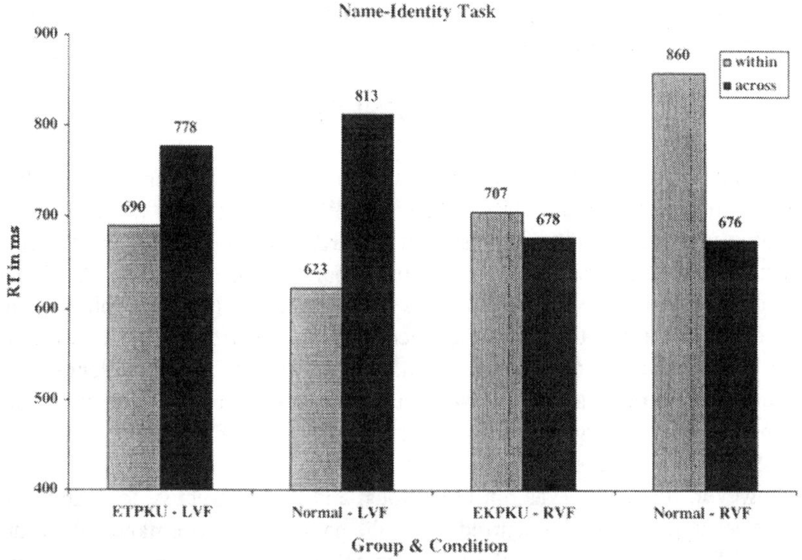

FIGURE 5 Median reaction time (RT) for the name-identity task. *Note.* ETPKU = early-treated phenylketonuria; LVF = left visual field matching probe; RVF = right visual field matching probe.

neurologically intact children (Banich, Passarotti, & Janes, this issue) and adults (Banich & Belger, 1990; Belger & Banich, 1992, 1998) suggest that the name-identity task typically yields an across-hemisphere advantage. Hence, the results in this study may represent a speed–accuracy trade-off for this group because the d' measure yielded neither a within- nor an across-hemisphere advantage.

For RVF-probe name-identity trials, the Group × Trial Type interaction approached but failed to reach significance ($p < .08$). Tests of simple effects revealed that for the ETPKU group there was neither a within- nor an across-hemisphere advantage ($p > .60$), whereas for the neurologically intact group there was a significant across-hemisphere advantage, $F(1, 18) = 12.68$, $p < .003$, which was consistent with the pattern we observed in a separate sample of neurologically intact children (Banich, Passarotti, & Janes, this issue). Hence, across both measures of performance, the groups appear to differ on RVF-probe name-identity trials, with the neurologically intact children showing a pattern similar to that obtained previously in adults (i.e., an across-hemisphere advantage) and the children with ETPKU not manifesting this pattern.

Once again, we performed tests of simple effects in an attempt to determine whether there were group differences in performance on RVF-probe name-identity trials. Contrary to what would be expected if there were left-hemisphere dysfunction in the ETPKU group, their RT was actually marginally significantly faster than that of the neurologically intact group, $F(1, 18) = 4.127, p < .06$, for within-hemisphere trials. No group differences were noted for across-hemisphere trials ($p > .98$).

DISCUSSION

The results of this study indicate that interhemispheric processing is less advantageous to children with ETPKU than to children who have no neurological compromise. Our results suggest that ETPKU has an additional effect on interhemispheric interaction beyond those reported in prior studies. Previously, Gourovitch et al. (1994) found deficits in the speed of interhemispheric transmission from the left to right hemisphere in children with ETPKU, as inferred from a Poffenberger (1912) paradigm, which requires simple integration of sensorimotor information. Our task, in contrast, was more cognitively demanding than the Poffenberger paradigm, but children with ETPKU also exhibited an atypical pattern of interhemispheric interaction.

However, this effect was not ubiquitous, and it is instructive to examine the conditions under which it occurred. First, the patterns of performance of children with ETPKU and of neurologically intact children did not differ for a computationally simple physical-identity task that typically yields a within-hemisphere advantage. Hence, no disruption in interhemispheric interaction was noted when such interaction was not particularly beneficial to task performance. However, when interhemispheric interaction would aid task performance, as was the case for the name-identity task, children with ETPKU did not exhibit the typical across-hemisphere interaction. Thus, it does not seem that their callosal functioning was affected under all conditions, but only when callosal channels were taxed and required for more efficient and accurate performance than was observed when all critical information was directed to a single hemisphere.

Second, the differences between neurologically intact children and those with ETPKU were most apparent for trials in which the left hemisphere made the match decision. Consistently across both the d' and RT measures for the RVF-probe trials, the children with ETPKU did not exhibit a significant across-hemisphere advantage, whereas the neurologically intact children did. This pattern may lead one to conclude that the deficit in interhemispheric interaction is asymmetric, a conclusion consistent with that of Gourovitch et al. (1994). However, there are reasons not to jump to such a conclusion. The data of the neurologically intact children on LVF-probe name-identity trials appear to be contaminated by a speed–accuracy trade-off, which means that these data do not provide a good baseline against which to evaluate whether the children with ETPKU have atypical interhemispheric interaction. Hence, as an exploratory analysis we compared performance on the name-identity task of children with ETPKU to that of a larger sample of neurologically intact children (Banich, Passarotti, & Janes, this issue) who were not matched for age and IQ. In this comparison, a difference between the children with ETPKU and the neurologically intact children was observed for LVF-probe name-identity trials, and once again the children with ETPKU failed to manifest an across-hemisphere advantage. Thus, rather than having specific left-hemisphere dysfunction, it may be that the deficit in children with ETPKU is apparent only under conditions in which an across-hemisphere advantage is obtained in neurologically intact children.

There are other reasons to believe that the performance of children with ETPKU may not be limited to left-hemisphere trials. The pattern we observed does not map well onto the results of Gourovitch et al. (1994). In their study, children with ETPKU exhibited a specific deficit when the left hemisphere received the stimulus and the right hemisphere generated the response. In contrast, in our study the most consistent evidence for atypical interhemispheric processing in children with ETPKU was observed on RVF-probe trials in which the decision was subserved by the left hemisphere. For our results to accord well with those of Gourovitch et al., deficits would have had to be observed not on RVF-probe trials but rather on across-hemisphere LVF-probe trials in which the decision was subserved by the right hemisphere. Therefore, rather than positing an asymmetric effect, we believe that children with ETPKU are likely to exhibit deficits whenever across-hemisphere processing is particularly beneficial to task performance.

Another issue we wished to address was whether there was a specific deficit in left-hemisphere functioning in children with ETPKU. Our data do not provide support for this notion. Our method allowed us to address this question in two separate manners. First, we were able to compare performance for the two groups of children on only those items in which all the critical sensory information was directed to the left hemisphere and in which the left hemisphere subserved a response (within RVF probe trials). Second, we were able to compare performance for the two groups of children on across-hemisphere RVF-probe items in which the critical sensory information was divided across the hemispheres, and in which the left hemisphere subserved a response. Neither of these comparisons provided any hint of a specific deficit in left-hemisphere processing for children with ETPKU, because their level of performance was not inferior to that of the neurologically intact children.

It is unclear which portion of the callosum is critical for performance of the Banich and Belger (1990) task. Copeland & Zaidel (1997) found that our interhemispheric tasks could not be performed by a split-brain patient with anterior section of the corpus callosum. Their findings suggest that the task is supported by callosal transfer of information between frontal regions. Hence, the deficits observed in the children with PKU may be related to frontal lobe function, which has a high degree of dopaminergic innervation. Although there is some recent evidence that the bilateral comparison of letters can be supported by the anterior commissure in acallosal individuals (Brown, Jeeves, Dietrich, & Burnison, 1999), we think it unlikely that this structure is playing the main role in our task in neurologically intact individuals. The anterior commissure appears to be able to support the transfer only of information that is relatively simple. For example, although a letter-matching task containing two sets of items can be performed in individuals without a corpus callosum but with an intact anterior commissure, a more complex pattern task cannot. We think that the complexity of our name-identity task exceeds that which can be supported by the anterior commissure.

In sum, our results provide evidence of atypical interhemispheric processing in children with ETPKU. However, this effect is not ubiquitous and only appears to emerge under conditions in which across-hemisphere processing is beneficial to performance. Thus, although basic interhemispheric processing mechanisms appear to be intact, children with ETPKU cannot accrue a performance advantage by dividing processing across the hemispheres under conditions of high computational complexity. It is possible that this inability may help to explain some of the other cognitive deficits observed in ETPKU. As reviewed by Banich (1998), interaction between the hemispheres appears to modulate and enhance a wide variety of attentional functions. It is noteworthy that attentional functioning is often compromised in individuals with PKU. For example, it has been reported that individuals with ETPKU have difficulties in sustained attention (e.g., Schmidt, Burgard, & Rupp, 1996; Schmidt et al., 1994). It is interesting to note that poorer callosal functioning in normal children has been linked to poor performance on sustained attention tasks (Rueckert & Levy, 1996; Rueckert, Sorenson, & Levy, 1994). Attentional deficits in ETPKU are not limited to sustained attention and have been found for other attentional tasks, such as the Stroop task (e.g., Weglage et al., 1996). Both lesion studies (e.g., Vendrell et al., 1995) and neuroimaging studies (e.g., Banich et al., 2000; Bench et al., 1993; Carter, Mintun, & Cohen, 1995) suggest that attentional selection in the Stroop task relies in part on the prefrontal cortex. Disruptions in interhemispheric interaction may also explain some of these effects in children with ETPKU, as we have found that interhemispheric interaction can modulate Stroop performance (Shenker & Banich, 2000). Future studies may fruitfully explore the relation between deficits in attentional functioning and interhemispheric interaction on tasks such as these.

ACKNOWLEDGMENTS

Portions of this research project were supported by Grant R01 MH 54217 from the National Institute of Mental Health to the Marie T. Banich.

We thank S. Bruce Dowton, Anne Hing, Carol Mantia, and Keiko Ueda for their generous contributions to recruitment and medical characterization of children with early-treated phenylketonuria. We also thank Ryan Calong, Betsy, Leritz, Tammy Mandernach, and Micah Rose for their contributions to data collection and data management. Finally, we thank Warren S. Brown for many helpful comments on previous versions of the article.

REFERENCES

Banich, M. T. (1995). Interhemispheric interaction: Mechanisms of unified processing. In F. L. Kitterle (Ed.), *Hemispheric communication: Mechanisms and models* (pp. 271–300). Hillsdale, NJ: Lawrence Erlbaum Associates, Inc.

Banich, M. T. (1998). The missing link: The role of interhemispheric interaction in attentional processing. *Brain and Cognition, 36,* 128–157.

Banich, M. T., & Belger, A. (1990). Interhemispheric interaction: How do the hemispheres divide and conquer a task? *Cortex, 26,* 77–94.

Banich, M. T., Milham, M. P., Atchley, R. A., Cohen, N. J., Webb, A., Wszalek, T., Kramer, A. F., Liang, Z.-P., Wright, A., Shenker, J., Magin, R., Barad, V., Gullett, D., Shah, C., & Brown, C. (2000). fMRI studies of Stroop tasks reveal unique roles of anterior and posterior brain systems in attentional selection. *Journal of Cognitive Neuroscience, 12,* 1–13.

Banich, M. T., & Shenker, J. I. (1994). Investigations of interhemispheric processing: Methodological considerations. *Neuropsychology, 8,* 263–277.

Banich, M. T., Stolar, N., Heller, W., & Goldman, R. (1992). A deficit in right-hemisphere performance after induction of a depressed mood. *Neuropsychiatry, Neuropsychology, and Behavioral Neurology, 5,* 20–27.

Banich, M. T., Passarotti, A. M., & Janes, D. (2000/this issue). Interhemispheric interaction during childhood: I. Neurologically intact children. *Developmental Neuropsychology, 18,* 33–51.

Bauman, M. L., & Kemper, T. L. (1982). Morphologic and histo-anatomic observations of the brain in untreated human phenylketonuria. *Acta Neuropathologica, 58,* 55–63.

Belger, A., & Banich, M. T. (1992). Interhemispheric interaction affected by computational complexity. *Neuropsychologia, 30,* 923–931.

Belger, A., & Banich, M. T. (1998). Costs and benefits of integrating information between the cerebral hemispheres: A computational perspective. *Neuropsychology, 12,* 380–398.

Bench, C. J., Frith, C. D., Grasby, P. M., Friston, K. J., Paulesu, E., Frackowiak, R. S. J., & Dolan, R. J. (1993). Investigations of the functional anatomy of attention using the Stroop test. *Neuropsychologia, 31,* 907–922.

Bick, U., Fahrendorf, G., Ludolph, A. C., Vassallo, P., Weglage, J., & Ullrich, K. (1991). Disturbed myelination in patients with treated hyperphenylalaninaemia: Evaluation with magnetic resonance imaging. *European Journal of Pediatrics, 150,* 185–189.

Bickel, H., Gerrard, J., & Hicksman, E. M. (1954). The influence of phenylalanine intake on the chemistry and behavior of a phenylketonuric child. *Acta Paediatrica, 43,* 64–77.

Brown, W. S., Jeeves, M. A., Dietrich, R., & Burnison, D. S. (1999). Bilateral field advantage and evoked potential interhemispheric transmission in commissurotomy and callosal agenesis. *Neuropsychologia, 37,* 1165–1180.

Carter, C., Mintun, M., & Cohen, J. D. (1995). Interference and facilitation effects during selection attention: An $H_2{}^{15}O$ PET study of Stroop task performance. *Neuroimage, 2,* 264–272.

Copeland, S. A., & Zaidel, E. (1997). Callosal channels and the bilateral distribution advantage: Patterns in agenesis and partial section of the corpus callosum [Abstract]. *Journal of the International Neuropsychological Society, 3,* 50.

Craft, S., Gourovitch, M. L., Dowton, S. B., Swanson, J. M., & Bonforte, S. (1992). Lateralized deficits in visual attention in males with developmental dopamine depletion. *Neuropsychologia, 30,* 341–351.

Diamond, A., & Herzberg, C. (1996). Impaired sensitivity to visual contrast in children treated early and continuously for phenylketonuria. *Brain, 119,* 523–538.

Diamond, A., Prevor, M. B., Callender, G., & Druin, D. P. (1997). Prefrontal cortex cognitive deficits in children treated early and continuously for PKU. *Monographs of the Society for Research in Child Development, 62,* 1–205.

Dobson, J. C., Kushida, E., Williamson, M., Friedman, E. G. (1976). Intellectual performance of 36 phenylketonuria patients and their nonaffected siblings. *Pediatrics, 58,* 53–58.

Dyer, C. A., Kendler, A., Philibotte, T., Gardiner, P., Cruz, J., & Levy, H. L. (1996). Evidence for central nervous system glial cell plasticity in phenylketonuria. *Journal of Neuropathology and Experimental Neurology, 55,* 795–814.

Giedd, J. N., Rumsey, J. M., Castellanos, F. X., Rajapakse, J. C., Kaysen, D., Vaituzis, A. C., Vauss, Y. C., Hamburger, S. D., & Rapoport, J. L. (1996). A quantitative MRI study of the corpus callosum in children and adolescents. *Developmental Brain Research, 91,* 274–280.

Gourovitch, M. L., Craft, S., Dowton, S. B., Ambrose, P., & Sparta, S. (1994). Interhemispheric transfer in children with early-treated phenylketonuria. *Journal of Clinical and Experimental Neuropsychology, 16,* 393–404.

Hudson, F. P., Mordaunt, V. L., & Leahy, I. (1970). Evaluation of treatment begun in the first three months of life in 184 cases of phenylketonuria. *Archives of Disease in Childhood, 45,* 5–12.

Kinsbourne, M. (1993). Orientation bias model of unilateral neglect: Evidence from attentional gradients within hemispace. In I. H. Roberson & J. C. Marshall (Eds.), *Unilateral neglect: Clinical and experimental studies* (pp. 63–86). Hove, England: Erlbaum.

Koch, R., Azen, C., Friedman, E. G., & Williamson, M. L. (1982). Preliminary report on the effects of diet discontinuation in PKU. *Pediatrics, 100,* 870–875.

Krause, W. L., Halmanaki, M., McDonald, L., Dembure, P., Salvo, R., Freides, D., & Elsas, L. J. (1985). Biochemical and neuropsychological effects of elevated plasma phenylalanine levels in patients with treated phenylketonuria. *Journal of Clinical Investigations, 75,* 40–48.

Ladavas, E., Nicoletti, R., Umilta, C., & Rizzolatti, G. (1984). Right hemisphere interference during negative affect: A reaction time study. *Neuropsychologia, 22,* 479–485.

Lund, E., & Wamberg, E. (1970). Phenylketonuria in Denmark. A screening programme 1962–1968. *Danish Medical Bulletin, 17,* 13–18.

Macombe, P. A., McLaughlin, D. B., Chalk, J. B., Brown, N. N., McGill, J. J., & Pender, M. P. (1992). Spasticity and white matter abnormalities in adult phenylketonuria. *Journal of Neuropathology and Experimental Neurology, 25,* 254–268.

Poffenberger, A. T. (1912). Reaction time to retinal stimulation with special reference to time lost in conducation through nerve centers. *Archives of Psychology (NY), 23,* 1–73.

Posner, M. I., Inhoff, A. W., Friedrich, F. J., & Cohen, A. (1987). Isolating attentional systems: A cognitive-anatomical analysis. *Psychobiology, 15,* 107–121.

Reynolds, R., Burri, R., Mahal, S., & Herschkowitz, N. (1992). Disturbed myelognsis and recovery in hyperphenylalaninemia in rats: An immunohistochemical study. *Experimental Neurology, 115,* 347–367.

Rueckert, L., & Levy, J. (1996). Further evidence that the callosum is involved in sustaining attention. *Neuropsychologia, 34,* 927–935.

Rueckert, L., Sorensen, L., & Levy, J. (1994). Callosal efficiency is related to sustained attention. *Neuropsychologia, 32,* 159–173.

Schmidt, E., Burgard, P., & Rupp, A. (1996). Effects of concurrent phenylalanine levels on sustained attention and calculation speed in patients treated early for phenylketonuria. *European Journal of Pediatrics, 155*(Suppl. 1), S82–S86.

Schmidt, E., Rupp, A., Burgard, P., Pietz, J., Weglage, J., & de Sonneville, L. (1994). Sustained attention in adult phenylketonuria: The influence of the concurrent phenylalanine-blood-level. *Journal of Clinical and Experimental Neuropsychology, 16,* 681–688.

Shenker, J. I., & Banich, M. T. (2000). *The modulation of attentional capacity in the Stroop task by communication between the cerebral hemispheres.* Manuscript submitted for publication.

Smith, I., Beasley, M. G., & Ades, A. E. (1991). Effect on intelligence of relaxing the low phenylalanine diet in phenylketonuria. *Archives of Disease in Childhood, 66,* 311–316.

Smith, M. L., Klim, P., Mallozzi, E., & Hanley, W. B. (1996). A test of the frontal-specificity hypothesis in the cognitive performance of adults with phenylketonuria. *Developmental Neuropsychology, 12,* 327–341.

Starfield, B., & Holtzman, N. A. (1975). A comparison of effectiveness of screening for phenylketonuria in the United States, United Kingdom and Ireland. *New England Journal of Medicine, 293,* 118–121.

Thompson, A. J., Tillotson, S., Smith, I., Kendall, B., Moore, S. G., Brenton, D. P. (1993). Brain MRI changes in phenylketonuria. Associations with dietary status. *Brain, 116,* 811–821.

Tucker, D. M., & Williamson, P. A. (1984). Asymmetric neural control systems in human self-regulation. *Psychological Review, 91,* 185–215.

Vendrell, P., Junqué, C., Pujol, J., Jurado, M. A., Molet, J., & Grafman, J. (1995). The role of prefrontal regions in the Stroop task. *Neuropsychologia, 33,* 341–352.

Weglage, J., Pietsch, M., Funders, B., Koch, H. G., & Ullrich, K. (1996). Deficits in selective and sustained attention processes in early treated children with phenylketonuria—Result of impaired frontal lobe functions? *European Journal of Pediatrics, 155,* 200–204.

Weissman, D. H., & Banich, M. T. (1999). Global–local interference modulated by communication between the hemispheres. *Journal of Experimental Psychology: General, 128,* 283–308.

Woo, S. L. C., Lidsky, A. S., Güttler, F., Chandra, T., & Robson, K. J. H. (1983). Cloned human phenylalanine hydroxylase gene allows prenatal diagnosis and carrier detection of classical phenylketonuria. *Nature, 306,* 151–155.

Woodcock, R. W., & Johnson, M. B. (1989). *Woodcock–Johnson Psychoeducational Battery–Revised.* Itasca, IL: Riverside.

Yakovlev, P. I., & Lecours, A. R. (1967). The myelogenetic cycles of regional maturation of the brain. In A. Minkowski (Ed.), *Regional development of the brain in early life* (pp. 3–70). Oxford, England: Blackwell.

DEVELOPMENTAL NEUROPSYCHOLOGY, *18*(1), 73–94

Absence of Interhemispheric Transfer of Unilateral Visuomotor Learning in Young Children and Individuals With Agenesis of the Corpus Callosum

Anne-Josée Chicoine
Groupe de Recherche en Neuropsychologie Expérimentale
Université de Montréal

Luc Proteau
Département de Kinésiologie
Université de Montréal

Maryse Lassonde
Groupe de Recherche en Neuropsychologie Expérimentale
Université de Montréal

This study was undertaken to investigate the role of the corpus callosum in interhemispheric transfer of unilateral visuomotor learning. In the first experiment, the cross-manual performance of 4 callosal agenesis participants was compared to that of 4 age- and IQ-matched controls. In the second experiment, normal children of different ages (6–7 and 11–12 years) and adults were submitted to the same task to assess the impact of callosal maturation on interhemispheric transfer. Participants had to make aiming movements from a starting position toward either a central or a lateral target on the same side as the hand used, while maintaining central fixation. Prior to training, a pretest was performed with the hand contralateral to the hand used during learning. Participants were then submitted to a posttest with the untrained hand. All participants learned the unilateral aiming task in the learning phase, as evidenced by a reduction in spatial errors with an increasing number of practice trials. However,

Requests for reprints should be sent to Maryse Lassonde, Groupe de Recherche en Neuropsychologie Expérimentale, Université de Montréal, C.P. 6128, Succursale Centre-ville, Montréal, Québec, H3C 3J7, Canada. E-mail: maryse.lassonde@umontreal.ca

acallosal participants and children aged 6 to 7 years failed to transfer the acquired skill from the trained to the untrained hemisphere. These findings suggest that interhemispheric transfer of visuomotor skills cannot be assumed by other structures in the case of agenesis or morphological immaturity of the corpus callosum. The results further indicate that unilateral visuomotor learning leads to the formation of a single, unihemispheric engram in the absence, whether functional or anatomical, of the corpus callosum.

It is now widely recognized that the mature brain relies principally on the corpus callosum for communication and collaboration between the hemispheres. Animal studies have clearly shown that the corpus callosum is necessary for interhemispheric transfer of unilateral visual, tactile, or motor learning (e.g., Eacott & Gaffan, 1990; Ebner & Myers, 1962; Myers, 1956; Myers & Henson, 1960). In the same context, it has long been known that practice of a skilled motor act with one hand facilitates learning of the same skill with the opposite hand (Munn, 1932). Human studies of cross-manual transfer of finger lifting (Edwards & Elliott, 1987), finger maze learning (Ward, Alvis, Sanford, Dodson, & Pusakulich, 1989), and rotary pursuit task (Byrd, Gibson, & Gleason, 1986) have confirmed this notion. However, few studies have investigated the effect of callosal absence in tasks requiring transfer of visuomotor learning. In fact, investigations of interhemispheric transfer involving a motor component have usually been limited to tasks based on bimanual motor control rather than on cross-manual motor learning.

With regard to interhemispheric transfer of learning, split-brain participants have been found to show poor cross-manual performance on the rotary pursuit task (Zaidel & Sperry, 1977), a task in which participants are required to learn how to trace a given path as quickly and accurately as possible. Transection of the corpus callosum has also been found to abolish transfer of tactuomotor form-board learning from the dominant to the nondominant hand (Goldstein & Joynt, 1975). In this task, the participant has to place, without the benefit of vision, geometric shapes in the corresponding holes on a wooden board. The reduction of time between the first trial, performed with the dominant hand, and the second, performed with the other hand, indicates that transfer or learning has taken place. Deficits in tactuomotor transfer of form-board learning and kinesthetic maze learning have also been observed in individuals born without the callosal commissure (Ferris & Dorsen, 1975; Gott & Saul, 1978; Jeeves, 1979), but results obtained with those tests are controversial. In fact, some authors do report good transfer of tactuomotor performance between the hands using a simpler version of the task (Sauerwein, Lassonde, Cardu, & Geoffroy, 1981) and preserved transfer of stylus maze learning (Reynolds & Jeeves, 1977).

Tasks involving bimanual motor control have generally yielded more consistent findings. Typically, patients who have undergone surgical section of the commissures are deficient with respect to speed of bimanual coordination, and they have difficulties maintaining a continued sequence of rapid asynchronous pronation–supination motions with the forearms (Zaidel & Sperry, 1977). In addition, they show learning impairments for new bimanual motor skills that require continuous mutual monitoring of both hands and bilateral interdependent motor control (Preilowski, 1972; Zaidel & Sperry, 1977). Similarly, acallosals are reportedly clumsy and impaired with respect to speed when performing bimanual operations (Chiarello, 1980; Jeeves, 1965; Jeeves, Silver, & Jacobson, 1988; Sauerwein et al., 1981). In fact, acallosal participants show the same deficits as anterior commissurotomy patients in a bimanual tracking task requiring asymmetrical input from the two hands (Jeeves, Silver, & Jacobson, 1988). It is interesting to note that when 5- to 6-year-old children were submitted to the same bimanual task, they were as impaired as the acallosal participants, whereas older children showed no difficulties (Jeeves, Silver, & Milner, 1988; Steese-Seda, Brown, & Caetano, 1995). The latter finding is taken as evidence of reduced interhemispheric communication for sensorimotor functions in cases of congenital absence or morphological immaturity of the corpus callosum.

It has often been proposed that the functional maturity of the corpus callosum coincides with the termination of its myelination cycle (Galin, Johnaston, Nakel, & Herron, 1979; Lassonde, Sauerwein, Chicoine, & Geoffroy, 1991; Quinn & Geffen, 1986). As anatomical work (Giedd et al., 1996; Yakovlev & Lecours, 1967) has shown, although the myelination of the callosal fibers is substantially advanced by the age of 6 years, this process continues until the age of 10 and even beyond. Furthermore, several behavioral studies addressing the issue of ontogeny of interhemispheric communication suggest a correlation between morphological and functional maturity. Increased efficiency of callosal transmission during ontogeny has indeed been inferred from tasks of cross-matching of tactile information (Galin et al., 1979; Lassonde et al., 1991), cross-localization of tactile stimulation (Galin, Diamond, & Herron, 1977; Hatta & Moriya, 1988; Lassonde et al., 1991; Quinn & Geffen, 1986), and cross-manual reproduction of a linear motor movement (O'Leary, 1980).

A developmental improvement in motor coordination has also been reported. Although bimanual mirror image movements are well executed at an early age (4 years), bimanual alternate supination–pronation movements seem to develop at a slower pace. It is not before the age of 8.5 years that adequate performance is observed, reflecting increased callosal efficiency (Njiokiktjien, Driessen, & Habraken, 1986). As for the development of interhemispheric transfer of sensorimotor learning, the only available data are derived from the Tactual Performance Test (Reitan & Davidson, 1974). These results indicate a tendency of older children to benefit more than younger ones from initial learning. In fact, 5- to 8-year-old children have been found to show limited cross-manual transfer of tactuomotor learning (Finlayson, 1976).

Taken together, these studies indicate that the ability of children to effect interhemispheric transfer develops progressively as a function of callosal maturation. The evidence further suggests that compensation for the functional absence of the corpus callosum, whether from congenital or developmental causes, is limited, especially when a motor component is involved. However, although there is some evidence that young children and acallosals are deficient with respect to bimanual motor coordination (Silver & Jeeves, 1994), no systematic study has been carried out to investigate their capacities of intermanually transferring a sensorimotor task that has been learned through practice and training.

This work was undertaken to extend the study of interhemispheric transfer to tasks involving unilateral visuomotor learning in cases of congenital absence as well as of morphological immaturity of the corpus callosum. Acallosals, neurologically intact children, and adults were required to learn to execute as precisely as possible aiming movements from a starting position toward either the middle or the side target ipsilateral to the hand used, while maintaining central fixation. Subsequently, intermanual transfer of the learned aiming movements was tested. In light of previous findings, we expected acallosals and young children to be deficient on the transfer task. We further predicted an improvement of cross-manual performance in the children with increasing age.

EXPERIMENT 1: CALLOSAL AGENESIS STUDY

Method

Participants

Four callosal agenesis participants and 4 control participants were part of this study. The demographic characteristics of the participants are presented in Table 1.

The first 2 participants, 1 left-handed man (M.G.) and his right-handed sister (L.G.), have been extensively described elsewhere (Lassonde, Sauerwein,

TABLE 1
Demographic Characteristics of the Acallosal and IQ-Matched Participants

Participants	*Sex*	*Age at Testing*	*IQ*	*Manual Dominance*
Acallosal				
M.G.	Male	22	78	Left
L.G.	Female	30	78	Right
S.G.	Female	31	84	Right
S.B.	Male	17	68	Right
Control				
R.O.	Male	24	82	Left
P.G.	Female	28	80	Right
A.R.M.	Female	33	81	Right
P.B.	Male	19	72	Right

McCabe, Laurencelle, & Geoffroy, 1988; Sauerwein et al., 1981). In both of these individuals, complete agenesis of the corpus callosum had first been diagnosed by pneumoencephalography and later confirmed by computer tomography (M.G. and L.G.) and by magnetic resonance in L.G. Both scored an IQ of 78 on the revised version of the Wechsler Adult Intelligence Scale (WAIS–R; Wechsler, 1981). At the time of testing, M.G. was 22 years old and L. G. was 30 years old.

The third participant (S.G.) is the oldest sister of the 2 participants just described. She was diagnosed following computer tomography scans administered to assess the distribution of the congenital abnormality in the family. S.G. is a 31-year-old, right-handed woman without any other known neurological pathology. She obtained a global IQ of 84 on the WAIS–R and has graduated from high school.

S.B. is a 17-year-old, right-handed boy who started to experience absence seizures accompanied by manual and buccal automatisms at the age of 6. Electroencephalogram data showed a rapid low-frequency dysrhythmia and some slow spikes over the temporal region of the left hemisphere. A computer tomography performed at the same time revealed complete agenesis of the corpus callosum. The seizures are presently well controlled with carbamazepine. S.B. obtained a global IQ of 68 on the revised version of the Wechsler Intelligence Scale for Children (WISC–R; Wechsler, 1974). He has completed his formal schooling and is presently unemployed.

The control group consisted of 4 participants without any documented neurological deficits but with a familial history of lower than average intellectual performances. They were matched with acallosal participants on the basis of age, sex, handedness, and IQ. Informed consent was obtained from all participants.

Task and Apparatus

The participants' task was to point with a stylus to one of two spatial targets (central or lateral) with the hand ipsilateral to the visual field that received the stimulus (input and output in the same hemisphere). To ensure that visual input reached only the designated hemisphere, participants had to maintain their gaze at all times on a central fixation point (see Figure 1). Except for some minor modifications, the pointing apparatus was similar to the one used by Chicoine, Proteau, and Lassonde (1992). It consisted of a horizontal wooden plate, measuring 40 cm × 20 cm, which contained a starting position, three targets, and a fixation point. The starting position was in line with the participant's sternum and consisted of a square copper plate on which a hand-held stylus could be placed. The back and side edges of the copper plate were 2 mm thicker than the center portion, making it easier to keep the stylus in contact with it. The starting position was located away from the middle target at 35 cm for the adults and at 25 cm for the children. At these distances, the arm and the forearm of the partic-

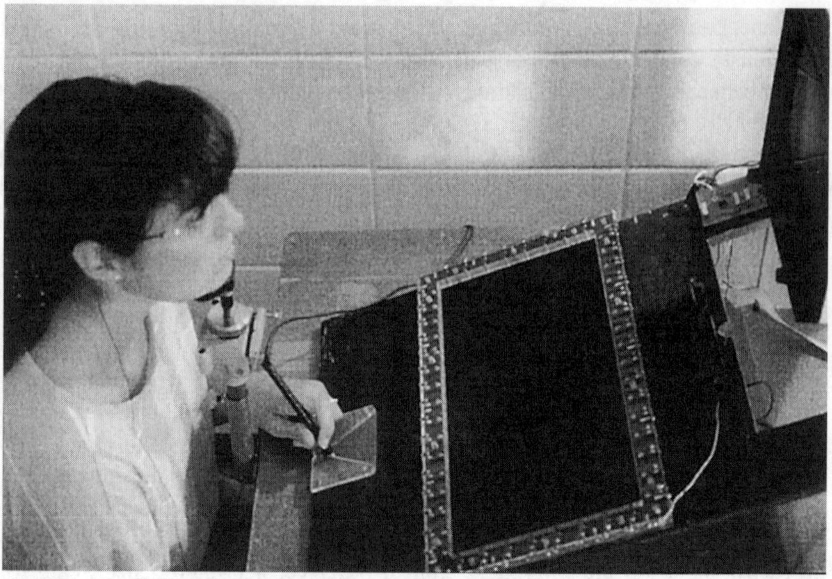

FIGURE 1 Schematic representation of the setup.

ipants formed an angle of 115° to 125° when hitting the middle target. The middle target was located at the center of the horizontal plate; the lateral targets were located at 10° of eccentricity to the left and to the right of the central target. The central fixation point was located 2.5 cm above the central target. The targets were composed of three filtered red light-emitting diodes (LED) of a small diameter (0.5 mm), whereas the fixation point was a bicolor LED (red–green).

The plate was covered by Teledeltos Recording Paper (Western Union Telegraph, model L-62s) and tilted 20° toward the participant to ensure that the targets were easily visible. This paper is isotropic resistive, and, when fed by a current alternately switched on its two axes, it allows for the spatial accuracy of a movement to be measured. To that end, a 12-bit analog-to-digital converter was used, providing the spatial accuracy of the endpoint movement to the nearest millimeter in the frontal (the x-axis) and the sagittal (the y-axis) planes. A 30-cm monochrome screen was placed on a platform over the pointing apparatus at eye level. This screen displayed three fixed dots, which represented the different targets, and a flashing dot, which indicated to the participant the locus where the stylus touched the target area after each trial. This latter information provided knowledge of results to the participants. The stylus was 16 cm long and weighed 80 g. Movement time was defined as the time taken between leaving the starting position and making contact with the target area.

The participants' horizontal eye movements were recorded using three skin electrodes, two fixed on the temporal and nasal sides of the right eye and a third one (ground) on the forehead. Electrooculogram (EOG) signals were amplified by a DC-Grass amplifier (model 7P1G) and displayed throughout the experiment on a Tektronix scope (model 5116). The signals were collected at a frequency of 500 Hz via a 12-bit analog-to-digital converter. Aiming errors (in millimeters) and movement time (in milliseconds) were recorded throughout the experiment. Stimulus and feedback presentation, as well as EOG monitoring and data collection, were controlled by an Apple IIe microcomputer.

Procedure

The participant was seated in front of the pointing apparatus in a darkened room, with the head held in place by an adjustable chinrest. The experiment took place in a single session and consisted of a graded practice phase and three experimental phases. Before the practice phase began, baseline EOG values were recorded at central and lateral target locations. These values were later used to ensure that lateral eye movements did not exceed 4° of eccentricity while executing the aiming movement.

The goal of the practice phase was to train the participant to maintain central fixation while performing the aiming movement. The practice comprised three different subphases. In a first phase, on naming the color of the fixation point (red or green), participants were asked to verbally identify which target was lit (left, center, or right) without making any eye movements. Once the naming task had been performed well, participants were invited to make aiming movements toward the intended target using their index finger, once again without moving their eyes. This procedure was practiced with each hand. Only after the finger task was mastered were the participants allowed to execute the aiming task with the stylus. The number of trials administered for each step of the practice phase depended on each participant's ability to follow the instructions. In general, about seven trials were necessary in each subphase.

The three experimental phases consisted of

1. A pretest, carried out with the left hand and composed of two blocks of 12 trials without knowledge of results; during the pretest, the left hand had to reach either the central or the left-sided target.
2. A learning phase, conducted with the right hand and consisting of eight blocks of 12 trials, with knowledge of results following each trial. The learning phase involved movements toward either the central or the right-sided target. Two targets were used during the learning phase to render the task difficult enough to require extended learning before reaching a ceiling level.

3. A subsequent posttest, performed with the untrained left hand, which was identical to the pretest.

Each experimental phase was followed by a 2-min rest period. All participants were required to perform pre- and posttests with their left hands and to use their right hands during learning. The left hand was chosen for both pre- and posttests because it was argued that, being the nondominant hand for most of the experimental and control participants, it was less apt than the right hand, and its imprecision thus left more room for interhemispheric transfer of learning to take place.

At the beginning of each trial, the participant placed the stylus at the starting position. Following a 2-sec delay, the fixation point was activated and the participant had to verbally identify its color. On correct identification, the target was activated, indicating to the participant that a movement could start. No emphasis was put on speed of response. The participants were only instructed to point the tip of the stylus to the target in a movement time ranging from 500 msec to 600 msec while maintaining central fixation. The purpose of having the participants perform their aiming movements within such a bandwidth was to avoid a speed–accuracy trade-off, with the emphasis being placed on precision rather than speed. If lateral eye movements exceeding 4° were detected on the initiation or during the execution of the movement, a computer-generated sound informed the participant that eye movements had occurred and that the trial was invalid. Such aborted trials were rerun randomly across the remaining trials. If the observed movement time fell outside the prescribed bandwidth, the participants were asked to execute their responses either faster or slower on the next trial. Once the pointing movement was completed, the turning off of the target light indicated to participants that they should return the stylus to the starting position. The targets were presented randomly in the central or the lateral position ipsilateral to the hand used to execute the task. During learning, knowledge of results was provided to the participants following each trial. Specifically, on completion of the movement, participants were invited to look at the monitor screen, which displayed three fixed dots representing the different targets and a flashing dot that indicated to participants the locus where the stylus touched the target area after each trial. This latter information provided knowledge of results to the participants.

Results

Statistical Analyses

Statistical analyses were carried out on the root mean square error (RMSE) for the spatial accuracy data (x- and y-axes, $\left(\sqrt{x_i^2 + y_i^2}\right)$) because this dependent variable represents the best overall measure of performance accuracy (Henry,

1975). To ensure that both acallosals and controls were able to respond within the prescribed bandwidth and that no speed–accuracy trade-off was present, an analysis was also carried out on movement times. For the temporal component of the task, the analyses were computed on the mean movement time.

Within-Hemisphere Learning

The results obtained during unimanual learning performed with the right hand were submitted to a three-way analysis of variance (ANOVA), with *groups* (acallosal vs. IQ-matched) as a between-subject variable and with *target* (central vs. lateral) and *blocks* (eight blocks of 12 trials each) as within-subjects variables. Separate analyses were performed for aiming accuracy (in millimeters) and movement time (in milliseconds).

The ANOVA performed on aiming accuracy revealed a significant main effect of learning, $F(7, 42) = 4.11, p < .05$ (block factor). As can be seen in Figure 2 (top), both the acallosal and the IQ-matched participants learned the task, as shown by improved performance with increasing amount of practice. In fact, the acallosals showed a 19% reduction in errors (first two blocks of practice – last two blocks of practice/first two blocks of practice), and the IQ-matched controls had an 8.4% reduction in errors. Because Figure 2 (top) tends to suggest a difference in the initial performance of the acallosals and their controls, post hoc comparisons using the Newman–Keuls technique ($p < .05$) were carried out. Results showed no significant difference in aiming precision between these two groups on the first three blocks of trials, nor did any other effect reach significance.

The results obtained on movement time are illustrated in Figure 2 (bottom). The ANOVA yielded a significant main effect of learning, $F(7, 42) = 3.65, p < .05$ (block effect), showing that all participants produced longer movement times with increased practice. However, it should be noted that this finding does not imply that the participants did not learn the task. It merely reflects the fact that they had difficulties executing the movement within the prescribed bandwidth, perhaps because of fatigue effects, because this finding was observed for the last blocks of trials. To ensure that the two groups did not differ during these last practice trials, Newman–Keuls post hoc comparisons ($p < .05$) were carried out. No significant differences were found between the acallosals and their IQ-matched controls on these last blocks of trials.

Interhemispheric Transfer of Learning

Two measures of interhemispheric transfer were computed. First, to verify whether the untrained hand benefited from the learning of the other hand, the results obtained with the left hand before (pretest) and after (posttest) learning with the right hand were compared (see Figure 3, top). A significant difference between

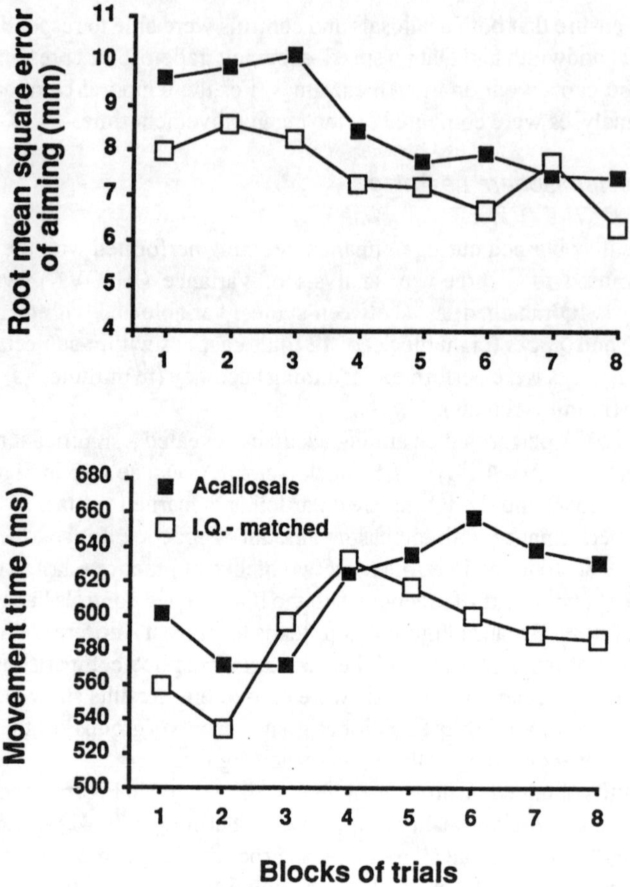

FIGURE 2 (Top) Root mean square error and (bottom) mean movement time as a function of training and groups (acallosals and IQ-matched controls).

these two measures was taken as indicating interhemispheric transfer of learning. A second measure of transfer was computed. The last two blocks of the learning phase, reflecting each participant's accuracy after learning (the participant's ceiling level) with the right hand, were also compared to the posttest carried out by the untrained left hand, and a minimal difference between these two values was taken to indicate that the untrained hand had benefited from the learning of the other hand (see Figure 3, bottom).

Left-hand performance before and after training of the right hand. The two dependent variables (movement time and aiming accuracy) were individually submitted to a three-way ANOVA, with *groups* (acallosals vs. IQ-matched) as a between-subject variable and with *target* (central vs. lateral) and *transfer test* (pretest vs. posttest) as within-subjects variables (see Figure 3, top).

The analysis for movement time showed that all participants obtained equivalent movement times on the pre- and posttests. Both groups of participants performed the task within the prescribed bandwidth before (controls, 560.7 msec;

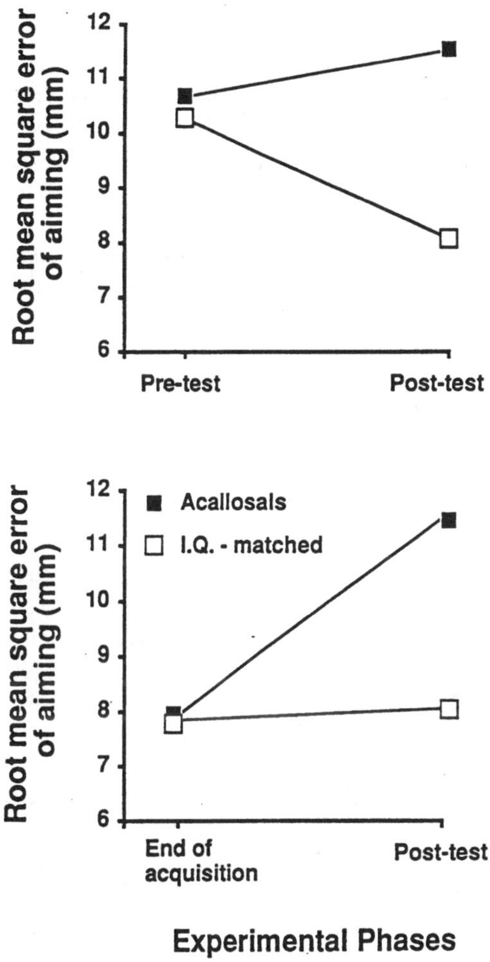

FIGURE 3 (Top) Root mean square error on the pretest and posttest and (bottom) root mean square error obtained on the last two blocks of learning versus that obtained on the posttest, as a function of groups (acallosals and IQ-matched controls).

acallosals, 572.2 msec) and after learning occurred with the right hand (controls, 554.3 msec; acallosals, 564.3 msec).

The results obtained on aiming accuracy revealed a significant main effect of target, $F(1, 6) = 28.55$, $p < .05$, showing that all participants were more precise when pointing to the central (mean RMSE of 8.06) rather than to the lateral target (mean RMSE of 10.15). The interaction between groups and transfer test, $F(1, 6) = 8.56$, $p < .05$, was also significant. Broken down into its simple effects, it revealed that aiming accuracy was similar for both groups on the pretest, whereas on the posttest a difference was found in the way each group performed the task. The IQ-matched participants improved by 17% (pretest – posttest/pretest) their aiming accuracy, $F(1, 6) = 12.16$, $p < .05$, but the acallosals displayed a 5.4% increase in errors in the posttest, $F(1, 6) = 0.43$, *ns* (see Figure 3, top). These findings indicate that interhemispheric transfer of learning occurred in the IQ-matched controls but not in the acallosal participants.

Transfer of learning from the trained to the untrained hand. To further explore the presence or absence of interhemispheric transfer, an additional three-way ANOVA was performed on aiming accuracy, with *groups* (acallosals vs. IQ-matched) as a between-subject variable and with *target* (central vs. lateral) and *experimental phases* (last two blocks of learning, right hand vs. posttest, left hand) as within-subjects variables (see Figure 3, bottom). A significant main effect of target was found, $F(1, 6) = 19.80$, $p < .05$., indicating better aiming accuracy on the central (mean RMSE of 7.17) than on the lateral target (mean RMSE of 8.85). As illustrated in Figure 3 (bottom), the interaction between groups and experimental phases showed that aiming accuracy was similar for both groups at the end of the learning phase, whereas on the posttest a significant difference was found showing that the IQ-matched participants were as accurate on the posttest as at the end of the learning phase, $F(1, 6) = 0.58$, *ns*, whereas the acallosals failed to reach, on the posttest, the level of accuracy obtained during the last two blocks of the learning phase $F(1, 6) = 13.25$, $p < .05$.

EXPERIMENT 2: DEVELOPMENTAL STUDY

Method

Participants

Forty normal right-handed children were divided into two groups according to their age: (a) 20 6- to 7-year-olds (mean age 7.1 years) and (b) 20 11- to 12-year-olds (mean age 12.1 years). A third group was composed of 20 right-handed adults (20–30 years old, mean age 27.8 years). A supplementary control study involved an additional group of 20 adults divided into two subgroups, one receiving training between pre- and posttests and the other undergoing a rest period between the two tests (no training; see the "Procedure" section that follows). Informed consent was obtained from all participants or their parents.

Task, Apparatus, and Procedure

The task and apparatus used in this experiment were the same as in the previous experiment. Furthermore, the time window of 500 msec to 600 msec was maintained because previous work, using a similar procedure, had shown that even the youngest group was able to respond adequately within these time limits (Chicoine et al., 1992). However, the procedure for the hand sequence in this study was randomized such that, in each of the three groups (6–7 years, 11–12 years, and adults), one half of the participants performed the pre- and posttests with their preferred right hand while using their nonpreferred hand during learning, and the other half followed the opposite hand sequence. As for the additional group of adults, one half of the participants executed the pre- and posttests without performing the learning phase. This phase was replaced by a pause of 30 min, which corresponded to the amount of time usually required to perform the learning phase. The other half of the participants executed all experimental phases.

Results

Within-Hemisphere Learning

The results obtained for aiming accuracy (in millimeters) and movement time (in milliseconds) were independently submitted to a four-way ANOVA, with *age* (6–7, 11–12, 20–30) and *hand used* (right vs. left) as between-subject variables and with *target* (central vs. lateral) and *blocks* (eight blocks of 12 trials each) as within-subjects variables.

The results regarding the spatial accuracy of the participants' aiming movement can be seen in Figure 4 (top). This figure illustrates significant main effects of age, $F(2, 54) = 42.87, p < .05$, and practice, $F(7, 378) = 9.28, p < .05$. Post hoc comparisons using the Newman–Keuls technique ($p < .05$) indicated that the younger participants (6–7 years old) were less accurate (mean RMSE of 10.05 mm) than the older ones (mean RMSEs of 7.37 mm and 7.00 mm for the 11- to 12-year-olds and the adults, respectively), but that aiming accuracy improved in all age groups with increasing practice. In fact, participants from the younger age group showed a 16% reduction in errors (first two blocks of practice – last two blocks of practice/first two blocks of practice), whereas the 11- to 12-year-olds and the adults, respectively, showed an 8.4% and a 9.1% reduction of errors. Significant main effects of hand, $F(1, 54) = 11.31, p < .05$, and target, $F(1, 54) = 23.68, p < .05$, were also found. Post hoc comparisons showed that all participants were more proficient with the right hand (mean RMSE of 7.65 mm vs. 9.18 mm), and that better aiming accuracy was obtained on the central target (mean RMSE of 7.71 mm vs. 8.58 mm). No other effect reached significance.

The analysis computed on movement time revealed a significant main effect of age, $F(2, 54) = 6.18, p < .05$, as well as a significant interaction between age and practice, $F(14, 378) = 3.05, p < .05$. This interaction is illustrated in Figure 4 (bottom). As can be seen from this figure, the younger children produced longer movement times on the first four blocks of trials, $F(2, 54) = 8.23$, 6.84, 6.49, and 4.37 for

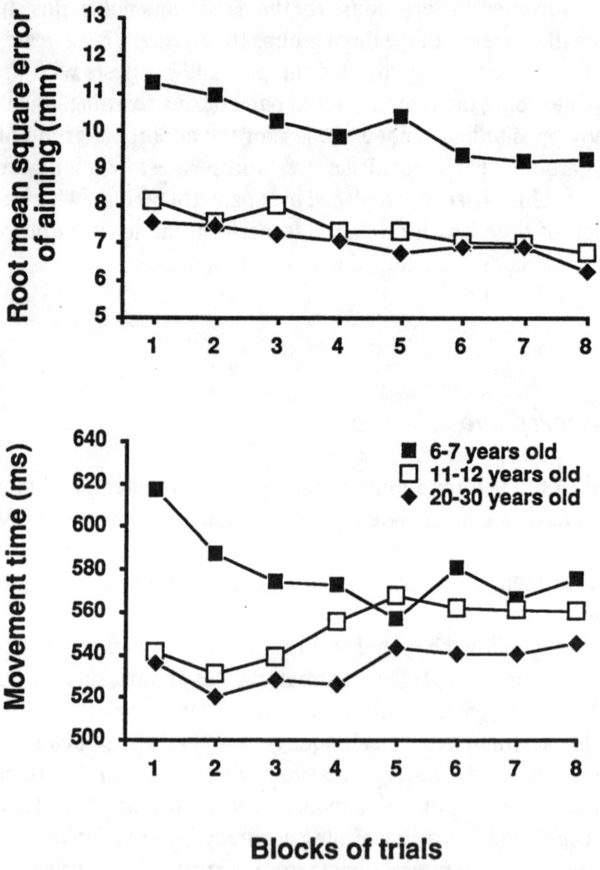

FIGURE 4 (Top) Root mean square error and (bottom) mean movement time as a function of training and age.

the first four blocks, respectively ($p < .05$), than the older participants. Thereafter, the young group performed the task within the prescribed bandwidth, as did the older groups. The results of this analysis confirm that all participants were able to complete their movements within the imposed time bandwidth and that the spatial accuracy data reported for the different age groups were not affected by different speed–accuracy trade-offs.

Interhemispheric Transfer of Learning

As in the previous study, two measures of interhemispheric transfer were computed. First, a comparison was carried out between the performance obtained by the untrained hand before (pretest) and after (posttest) training of the other hand. Second, the last two blocks of the learning phase, reflecting each participant's accuracy after learning (the participant's ceiling level) with the trained hand, were also compared to the posttest carried out by the untrained hand.

Performance of the untrained hand before and after training of the other hand. The two dependent variables (movement time and aiming accuracy) were submitted to separate four-way ANOVAs, with *age* (6–7, 11–12, 20–30) and *hand used* (right vs. left) as between-subject variables and with *target* (central vs. lateral) and *transfer test* (pre- vs. posttest) as within-subjects variables.

The analysis performed on movement time yielded significant main effects of age, $F(2, 54) = 13.46, p < .05$, and hand, $F(1, 54) = 30.03, p < 05$, as well as a significant interaction between age and hand, $F(2, 54) = 3.83, p < .05$. The simple effects of this interaction showed that the adults executed the pre- and posttests at the same speed with either hand, $F(1, 54) = 0.85$, *ns,* whereas the younger participants were significantly slower with the left than with the right hand, $F(1, 54) = 16.25$ and 20.58 for the 6- to 7-year-olds and 11- to 12-year-olds, respectively ($p < .05$). No significant differences in movement time were observed between the central and the lateral targets or between the pre- and posttests for any of these groups.

The ANOVA performed on aiming accuracy revealed a significant main effect of target, $F(1, 54) = 11.03, p < .05$, indicating better aiming accuracy on the central (mean RMSE of 8.05) than on the lateral target (mean RMSE of 8.87). More important, the results indicated that age, $F(2, 54) = 46.15, p < .05$; transfer test, $F(1, 54) = 11.59, p < .05$; and the interaction between these two factors, $F(2, 54) = 4.27$, $p < .05$, were significant. This interaction is illustrated in Figure 5 (top). It is apparent from this figure that the older participants (11–12 and 20–30 years old) were more accurate on the posttest than on the pretest, $F(1, 54) = 5.44$ and 14.63, respectively ($p < .05$), whereas the 6- to 7-year-old children showed no improvement in aiming accuracy between pre- and posttests, $F(1, 54) = 0.07$, *ns.*

Transfer of learning from the trained to the untrained hand. An additional four-way ANOVA was performed on aiming accuracy, with *age* (6–7, 11–12, 20–30) and *hand used* (right vs. left) as between-subject variables and with *target* (central vs. lateral) and *experimental phases* (last two blocks of learning vs. posttest) as within-subjects variables (see Figure 5, bottom). A significant main effect of target was found, $F(1, 54) = 5.56, p < .05$, showing that all participants were more precise when pointing to the central target (mean RMSE of 7.60) than to the lateral target (mean RMSE of 8.10). The analysis also revealed significant main ef-

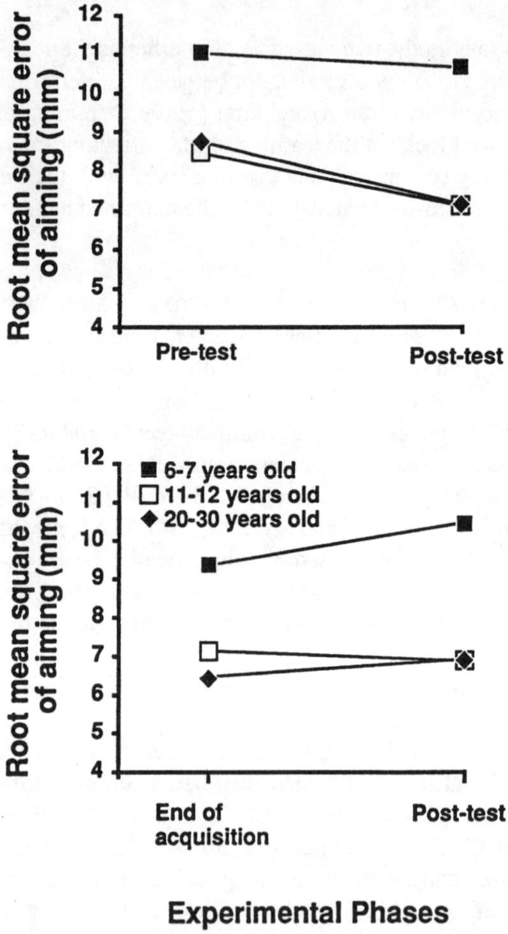

FIGURE 5 (Top) Root mean square error on the pretest and posttest and (bottom) root mean square error obtained on the last two blocks of learning versus that obtained on the posttest, as a function of age.

fects of age, $F(2, 54) = 55.19, p < .05$, and experimental phases, $F(1, 54) = 11.03, p < .05$. A significant interaction between age and experimental phases was also found. This interaction is illustrated in Figure 5 (bottom), which shows that there is no significant difference between aiming accuracy obtained at the end of the learning phase and on the posttest for the older participants and the adults, $F(1, 54) = 0.80$ and 1.36, for the 11- to 12-year-olds and for the adults, respectively, (*ns*), whereas the young group was significantly less accurate on the posttest than during the last two blocks of learning, $F(1, 54) = 13.55, p < .05$.

Supplementary Analyses

Because one objective of this study was to compare the interhemispheric performance of callosal agenesis patients to that of 6- to 7-year-old children, whose corpus callosum is presumably not fully functional, an additional two-way ANOVA was computed, with *groups* (acallosals vs. 6- to 7-year-olds) as a between-subject variable and with *transfer test* (pre- vs. posttest) as a within-subjects variable. The results showed no significant differences between these two groups. In fact, both groups obtained comparable levels of accuracy in the pre- and posttests, apparently not showing any transfer of learning.

Finally, an additional ANOVA was conducted, with *groups* (acallosals, trained and untrained adults) as a between-subject variable and with *transfer test* (pre- vs. posttest) as a within-subjects variable. The analysis revealed a significant main effect of group, $F(2, 21) = 4.51, p < .05$, as well as a significant interaction between group and transfer test, $F(2, 21) = 3.95, p < .05$. Broken down into its simple effects, this interaction showed that there was no improvement in aiming accuracy on the posttest for both the acallosals and untrained adults, $F(1, 21) = 0.63$ and 0.05, respectively (*ns*), as opposed to the trained adults, who showed significant increased precision on the posttest, $F(1, 21) = 4.41, p < .05$.

DISCUSSION

The most salient finding of this work was that both individuals born without the callosal commissure and normal young children were equally deficient on the interhemispheric transfer of a visuomotor learning task. Although all participants were perfectly able to learn the aiming task unilaterally, as evidenced by reduced spatial errors with practice, the acallosals and the young children failed to show cross-integration of sensorimotor activity, as revealed by their inability to benefit from the practice with one hand when the other hand was tested. In fact, the pre- and posttraining performances of the acallosals were indistinguishable from those observed in a group of adults submitted to the same tests without the intervening training.

Previous work conducted on the ontogeny of interhemispheric transfer in normal children has already underlined the progressive role of the corpus callosum in tasks that require cross-manual integration of tactile information (Galin et al., 1977; Galin et al., 1979; Lassonde et al., 1991; O'Leary, 1980; Quinn & Geffen, 1986). Our findings are in agreement with these earlier findings concerning the developmental aspects of interhemispheric transfer in normal children. The importance of this study is that the concept of increased interhemispheric transfer with age is also valid for tasks requiring visuomotor training.

In keeping with the hypothesis of callosal maturation, our findings show the expected progression of interhemispheric efficiency with increasing age. The results clearly demonstrate that children improve in their ability to transfer unilaterally learned aiming movements toward a visual target from the skilled to the untrained hand. Like the acallosal participants, the youngest children (6–7 years) showed no interhemispheric transfer of visuomotor learning, whereas the older children (11–12 years) were as proficient as the adults. The results suggest either that children may not be able to use their corpus callosum as efficiently as adults before the myelination cycle of this structure is complete or that they may rely on extracallosal pathways to carry this interhemispheric task (Lassonde et al., 1991). In fact, the finding that younger children, who have a corpus callosum, albeit an immature one, were as impaired as the acallosal participants, who rely on slower secondary commissures to achieve interhemispheric transfer, suggests that speed of transfer may be the determining factor in allowing the formation of a dual engram when one hemisphere is being trained.

One of the major roles of the corpus callosum may indeed be the rapid transfer of information between the hemispheres, a function that would keep each hemisphere instantly updated and able to respond to ongoing demands. This is especially important for tasks requiring a motor response under time constraints. Slowness has, in fact, been found to be one of the major limitations of cross-integration in acallosals and young children (Di Stefano, Sauerwein, & Lassonde, 1992; Lassonde et al., 1988; Lassonde et al., 1991). Earlier studies have also shown that acallosals and young children are clumsy in their performance of even simple skilled activities requiring bimanual coordination (Jeeves, 1965; Lassonde et al., 1991; Sauerwein et al., 1981). In addition, they show deficits comparable to those of split-brain patients in a bimanual tracking task that requires a simultaneous output from both hemispheres (Jeeves, Silver, & Jacobson, 1988; Jeeves, Silver, & Milner, 1988).

However, acallosal participants do show other types of visuomotor deficits that may not be easily attributable to a general slowness of cross-integration. For instance, they fail to show normal prehensile and aiming movements (Jakobson, Servos, Goodale, & Lassonde, 1994; Jeeves & Silver, 1988; Lassonde, 1994). Such failure to perform normally on tasks involving a motor component has often been linked to the preserved use of uncrossed ipsilateral motor pathways in acallosals. It has been postulated that reinforcement of ipsilateral output results from the absence, during development, of the normal inhibitory action of the corpus callosum on these projections (Dennis, 1976). Consequently, ipsilateral pathways would compete with contralateral output, producing motor deficits (Dennis, 1976; Jeeves, 1986, 1994). In further support of this hypothesis, Dennis reported that, when differentiated finger movements are mediated by uninhibited ipsilateral projections, unintended associated movements will occur. This author found that synkinesis within and between hands occurred more often in acallosal than in normal persons. Synkinesis can also be observed in cases of cerebral immaturity. Thus, children under the age of 10 years have been found to exhibit greater contralateral and ipsilateral motor overflow than adults when executing a task of independent movement control (Edwards & Elliott, 1987). A developmental decrease of synkinesis associated with bimanual alternate movements has also been reported between the ages of 4 and 9 years (Njiokiktjien et al., 1986). Such findings suggest that motor control in young children and in acallosal persons could be equally perturbed as a result of competition between ipsilateral and contralateral motor pathways. It is possible that such competition may equally hinder the formation of a dual engram during unimanual visuomotor training.

Cerebral immaturity may also account for the fact that the youngest children did not demonstrate the same level of precision as the older ones in the intramanual conditions. They did show learning of the task when it was carried out intrahemispherically, but they failed to transfer such learning to the other, untrained hemisphere. The acallosal participants, on the other hand, were able to learn the task intrahemispherically to the same degree of proficiency as their IQ-matched participants. Their problem clearly resided in transferring the learned response from the trained to the untrained hemisphere. Few disconnection deficits have been reported for callosal agenesis patients. Earlier findings have stressed the fact that these patients are usually able to compensate for the congenital absence of the corpus callosum, at least in the visual and tactile modalities (Ettlinger, Blakemore, Milner, & Wilson, 1972, 1974; Jeeves, 1965, 1986; Lassonde et al., 1988; Lassonde et al., 1991; Sauerwein & Lassonde, 1983; Sauerwein et al., 1981). Such preserved capacities in the absence of the largest commissure have been attributed to the use, through neural plasticity, of alternative pathways (for reviews, see Jeeves, 1986, 1994).

However, the absence of transfer of sensorimotor learning reinforces the notion that the compensatory mechanisms in the case of congenital absence of the corpus callosum, proposed by a number of authors, are effective primarily for transfer in the sensory modalities but that they seem to be inefficient when a motor component has to be transferred (Lassonde, 1994; Lassonde, Sauerwein, & Lepore, 1995). The absence of plasticity in motor cross-integration may be related to the fact that the cortical areas subserving distal motor control, namely the frontal lobes, do not reach their functional maturity before puberty (Huttenlocher, 1990).

In contrast to the regions that mediate the sensory modalities, the full maturation of the frontal lobes may take place after completion of the critical period of callosal plasticity, which would explain the limited adjustment to callosal absence in tasks requiring some motor control. In fact, the anterior part of the corpus callosum is the most likely region to be involved in visuomotor transfer. This assumption is based on the observation of a previous study, which showed that split-brain patients with sparing of the splenium of the corpus callosum were as impaired on a procedural task involving visuomotor learning as the completely callosotomized patients and callosal agenesis participants (de Guise et al., 1999).

Taken together, the results of the callosal and developmental studies emphasize the role of the principal neocortical commissure for interhemispheric transfer of unilateral visuomotor learning. Indeed, our results suggest that compensation for congenital or functional absence of the corpus callosum is extremely limited when cross-manual transfer of visuomotor skills is required. This finding questions the efficiency of the compensatory pathways as an alternative route for the integration and transfer of sensorimotor information.

ACKNOWLEDGMENTS

This study was supported by Grants OGPIN02510 and OGPIN00476 from the National Science and Engineering Research Council of Canada awarded to Maryse Lassonde and Luc Proteau and by Grant 02478 from the Ministère de l'Éducation du Québec awarded to Maryse Lassonde.

We thank Claude Brouillette and Pierre Black for the development of the hardware and software and Hannelor Sauerwein for her comments on the text.

REFERENCES

Byrd, R., Gibson, M., & Gleason, M. H. (1986). Bilateral transfer across ages 7 to 17 years. *Perceptual and Motor Skills, 62,* 87–89.

Chiarello, C. (1980). A house divided? Cognitive functioning with callosal agenesis. *Brain and Language, 11,* 128–158.

Chicoine, A. J., Proteau, L., & Lassonde, M. (1992). Developmental aspects of sensorimotor integration. *Developmental Neuropsychology, 8,* 381–394.

de Guise, E., Del Pesce, M., Foschi, N., Quattrini, A., Papo, I., & Lassonde, M. (1999). Callosal and cortical contribution to procedural learning. *Brain, 122,* 1049–1062.

Dennis, M. (1976). Impaired sensory and motor differentiation with the corpus callosum agenesis. A lack of inhibition during ontogeny? *Neuropsychologia, 14,* 455–469.

Di Stefano, M. R., Sauerwein, H. C., & Lassonde, M. (1992). Influence of anatomical factors and spatial compatibility on the stimulus–response relationship in the absence of the corpus callosum. *Neuropsychologia, 30,* 177–185.

Eacott, M. J., & Gaffan, D. (1990). Interhemispheric transfer of visuomotor conditional learning via the anterior corpus callosum of monkeys. *Behavioural Brain Research, 38,* 109–116.

Ebner, F. F., & Myers, R. E. (1962). Corpus callosum and the interhemispheric transmission of tactile learning. *Journal of Neurophysiology, 25,* 380–391.

Edwards, J. M., & Elliott, D. (1987). Effect of unimanual training on contralateral motor overflow in children and adults. *Developmental Neuropsychology, 3,* 299–309.

Ettlinger, G., Blakemore, C. B., Milner, A. D., & Wilson, J. (1972). Agenesis of the corpus callosum: A behavioural investigation. *Brain, 95,* 327–346.

Ettlinger, G., Blakemore, C. B., Milner, A. D., & Wilson, J. (1974). Agenesis of the corpus callosum: A further behavioural investigation. *Brain, 97,* 225–234.

Ferris, G. S., & Dorsen, M. M. (1975). Agenesis of the corpus callosum: Neuropsychological studies. *Cortex, 11,* 95–122.

Finlayson, M. A. J. (1976). A behavioral manifestation of the development of interhemispheric transfer of learning in children. *Cortex, 12,* 290–295.

Galin, D., Diamond, R., & Herron, J. (1977). Development of crossed and uncrossed tactile localization on the fingers. *Brain and Language, 4,* 588–590.

Galin, D., Johnaston, J., Nakel, L., & Herron, J. (1979). Development of the capacity for tactile information transfer between hemispheres in normal children. *Science, 204,* 1330–1332.

Giedd, J. N., Rumsey, J. M., Castellanos, F. X., Rajapakse, J. C., Kaysen, D., Vaituzis, A. C., Vauss, Y. C., Hamburger, S. D., & Rapoport, J. L. (1996). A quantitative MRI study of the corpus callosum in children and adolescents. *Brain Research, 91,* 274–280.

Goldstein, M. N., & Joynt, R. J. (1975). Long-term follow-up of a callosal-sectioned patient: Report of a second case. *Archives of Neurology, 32,* 52–53.

Gott, P. S., & Saul, R. E. (1978). Agenesis of the corpus callosum: Limits of functional compensation. *Neurology, 28,* 1272–1279.

Hatta, T., & Moriya, K. (1988). Developmental changes of hemisphere collaboration for tactile sequential information. *International Journal of Behavioral Development, 11,* 451–465.

Henry, F. M. (1975). Absolute error versus "E" in target accuracy. *Journal of Motor Behavior, 7,* 227–228.

Huttenlocher, P. (1990). Morphometric study of human cerebral cortex development. *Neuropsychologia, 28,* 517–527.

Jakobson, L., Servos, P., Goodale, M. A., & Lassonde, M. (1994). Control of proximal and distal components of prehension. *Brain, 117,* 1107–1113.

Jeeves, M. A. (1965). Psychological studies of three cases of congenital agenesis of the corpus callosum. In E. G. Ettlinger (Ed.), *Function of the corpus callosum* (pp. 73–94). London: Macmillan.

Jeeves, M. A. (1979). Some limits of interhemispheric integration in cases of callosal agenesis. In I. S. Russel, M. W. Van Hof, & G. Berlucchi (Eds.), *Structure and function of the cerebral commissures* (pp. 449–474). London: Macmillan.

Jeeves, M. A. (1986). Callosal agenesis: Neuronal and developmental adaptations. In F. Lepore, M. Ptito, & H. H. Jaspers (Eds.), *Two-hemispheres—one brain* (pp. 403–421). New York: Alan Liss.

Jeeves, M. A. (1994). Callosal agenesis—a natural split-brain overview. In M. Lassonde & M. A. Jeeves (Eds.), *Callosal agenesis—a natural split brain?* (pp. 285–300). New York: Plenum.

Jeeves, M. A., & Silver, P. H. (1988). The formation of finger grip during prehension in an acallosal patient. *Neuropsychologia, 26,* 153–159.

Jeeves, M. A., Silver, P. H., & Jacobson, L. (1988). Bimanual co-ordination in callosal agenesis and partial commissurotomy. *Neuropsychologia, 26,* 833–850.

Jeeves, M. A., Silver, P. H., & Milner, A. D. (1988). Role of the corpus callosum in the development of a bimanual motor skill. *Developmental Neuropsychology, 4,* 305–323.

Lassonde, M. (1994). Disconnection syndrome in callosal agenesis. In M. Lassonde & M. A. Jeeves (Eds.), *Callosal agenesis—a natural split brain?* (pp. 275–284). New York: Plenum.

Lassonde, M., Sauerwein, H., Chicoine, A. J., & Geoffroy, G. (1991). Absence of disconnexion syndrome in callosal agenesis and early callosotomy: Brain reorganization or lack of structural specificity during ontogeny? *Neuropsychologia, 29,* 481–495.

Lassonde, M., Sauerwein, H. C., & Lepore, F. (1995). Extent and limits of callosal plasticity: Presence of disconnection symptoms in callosal agenesis. *Neuropsychologia, 33,* 989–1007.

Lassonde, M., Sauerwein, H., McCabe, N., Laurencelle, L., & Geoffroy, G. (1988). Extent and limits of cerebral adjustment to early or congenital absence of the corpus callosum. *Behavioural Brain Research, 30,* 165–181.

Munn, N. L. (1932). Bilateral transfer of learning. *Journal of Experimental Psychology, 15,* 343–353.

Myers, R. E. (1956). Function of corpus callosum in interocular transfer. *Brain, 79,* 358–363.

Myers, R. E., & Henson, C. O. (1960). Role of the corpus callosum in transfer of tactuokinesthetic learning in chimpanzee. *Archives of Neurology, 3,* 404–409.

Njiokiktjien, C., Driessen, M., & Habraken, L. (1986). Development of supination–pronation movements in normal children. *Human Neurobiology, 5,* 199–203.

O'Leary, D. (1980). A developmental study of interhemispheric transfer in children five to ten. *Child Development, 51,* 743–750.

Preilowski, B. (1972). Possible contribution of the anterior forebrain commissures to bilateral motor coordination. *Neuropsychologia, 10,* 267–277.

Quinn, K., & Geffen, G. (1986). The development of tactile transfer of information. *Neuropsychologia, 24,* 793–804.

Reitan, R. W., & Davidson, L. A. (1974). *Clinical neuropsychology: Current status and application.* New York: Wiley.

Reynolds, M. D., & Jeeves, M. A. (1977). Further studies of tactile perception and motor coordination in agenesis of the corpus callosum. *Cortex, 13,* 257–272.

Sauerwein, H., & Lassonde, M. (1983). Intra- and interhemispheric processing of visual information in callosal agenesis. *Neuropsychologia, 21,* 167–171.

Sauerwein, H., Lassonde, M., Cardu, B., & Geoffroy, G. (1981). Interhemispheric integration of sensory and motor functions in agenesis of the corpus callosum. *Neuropsychologia, 19,* 445–454.

Silver, P. H., & Jeeves, M. A. (1994). Motor coordination in callosal agenesis. In M. Lassonde & M. A. Jeeves (Eds.), *Callosal agenesis—a natural split brain?* (pp. 207–220). New York: Plenum.

Steese-Seda, D., Brown, W., & Caetano, C. (1995). Development of visuomotor coordination in school-age children: The bimanual coordination test. *Developmental Neuropsychology, 11,* 181–199.

Ward, J. P., Alvis, G. R., Sanford, C. G., Dodson, D. L., & Pusakulich, R. L. (1989). Qualitative differences in tactuo-spatial motor learning by left-handers. *Neuropsychologia, 27,* 1091–1099.

Wechsler, D. (1974). *Manual for the Wechsler Intelligence Scale for Children–Revised.* San Antonio, TX: Psychological Corporation.

Wechsler, D. (1981). *Manual for the Wechsler Adult Intelligence Scale–Revised.* San Antonio, TX: Psychological Corporation.

Yakovlev, P., & Lecours, A. (1967). The myelogenic cycles of regional maturation of the brain. In A. Minowski (Ed.), *Regional development of the brain in early life* (pp. 3–70). Oxford, England: Blackwell.

Zaidel, D., & Sperry, R. W. (1977). Some long-term motor effects of cerebral commissurotomy in man. *Neuropsychologia, 10,* 103–110.

DEVELOPMENTAL NEUROPSYCHOLOGY, *18*(1), 95–112

Individual Differences in Neurobehavioral Measures of Laterality and Interhemispheric Function as Measured by Dichotic Listening

Patricia Cowell
Department of Human Communication Sciences
University of Sheffield, England

Kenneth Hugdahl
Department of Biological and Medical Psychology
University of Bergen, Norway

This article presents analysis of dichotic listening performance in 57 healthy men and women aged 20 to 72 years. The data are presented as a means to cover 2 theoretical issues relevant to the biobehavioral study of laterality and interhemispheric relations. First, the sensitivity of dichotic listening performance to factors such as sex, age, and their interactions was examined. Dichotic listening asymmetry scores were found to vary as a function of sex, age, handedness, and family history of developmental language disorders. The effects of sex and age were then explored in relation to a comparison of nonforced and unilaterally focused test conditions. The results suggest that even within a healthy, normative sample of human participants, individuals vary not only in their underlying perceptual asymmetries for auditory input, but also in the manner in which such asymmetries interact with other higher order cognitive functions.

There has been an enormous amount of controversy surrounding the reproducibility of structural and behavioral measures of laterality and interhemispheric function. In the area of human sex differences research, there have been very few stable effects found in studies of corpus callosum anatomy (Bishop & Wahlsten, 1997) or by using

---

Requests for reprints should be sent to Patricia Cowell, Department of Human Communication Sciences, University of Sheffield, 31 Claremont Crescent, Sheffield S10 2TA, England. Email: p.e.cowell@sheffield.ac.uk

behavioral measures such as dichotic listening (Hiscock, Inch, Jacek, Hiscock-Kalil, & Kalil, 1994) or the visual half-field technique (McKeever, 1986). As a result, some researchers have deemed these measures too variable and have questioned the need for further research. An alternative view is that these measures are highly sensitive to many developmental, physiological, and behavioral factors, which makes them ideal, rather than problematic, for use in the investigation of individual differences (Cowell, Denenberg, Boehm, Kertesz, & Nasrallah, in press).

The dependent measure selected as the basis of our analysis of individual differences is dichotic listening, a behavioral technique used to study brain asymmetry in auditory-phonetic processing that focuses on left–right differences in the perception of simple language stimuli (Bryden, 1988; Hugdahl, 1995). In the dichotic listening situation, the participant is presented with two different stimuli, one in each ear. The stimuli are typically computer generated to allow for optimal synchronization between the output channels. Thus, the basic feature of the dichotic situation is to provide more elements at any moment in time than the brain is capable of processing. The question then becomes which elements or components of the stimulus input will be selected. By further instructing the participant to focus attention on either the right or left ear input, effects of vigilance and attentional shifts can be studied within the same paradigm. The dichotic situation thus allows the experimenter not only to probe laterality differences in sensory-perceptual processing, but also to analyze dynamic cognitive effects. A typical finding in normal right-handed participants is the so-called right-ear advantage (REA), which means that more items are correctly reported from the right, compared to the left, ear. The REA in dichotic listening is believed to reflect the linguistic specialization of the left hemisphere. Conversely, absence of a REA (i.e., symmetry) or the presence of a left-ear advantage (LEA) may indicate either atypical organization or left temporal lobe dysfunction (Hugdahl, 1995). Using a version of the dichotic listening test that incorporates multiple behaviorocognitive dimensions allows for more in-depth analysis of the factors that contribute to variability across studies.

In the field of laterality and interhemispheric relations, studies often focus on one or two independent variables while not analyzing the data for factors that have been shown by other studies to affect the structure or function in question. For example, the anatomy of the corpus callosum has been shown to be sensitive to the interactive effects of sex and degree of right-hand preference (Cowell, Kertesz, & Denenberg, 1993; Habib et al., 1991; Witelson, 1989). In addition, there have been reports on the relation between regional callosal anatomy and the interactive effects of sex and age (Aboitiz, Rodriguez, Olivares, & Zaidel, 1996; Cowell, Allen, Zalatimo, & Denenberg, 1992). However, there is a tendency for the sex and handedness research to downplay the effects of age (Cowell et al., 1993; Habib et al., 1991; Witelson, 1989), and for the aging and development research to deemphasize the interactive effects of sex and handedness (Aboitiz et al., 1996; Cowell et al., 1992; Rauch & Jinkins, 1994). A similar argument can be made in the study of behavioral correlates of laterality and interhemispheric function. For example, Hiscock et al. (1994) reviewed the literature on sex differences in dichotic listening; many of the studies considered the handedness of participants and the nature of the stimuli, but there was little emphasis on age effects either within or across experiments.

There have also been numerous studies examining group differences in measures of laterality and of interhemispheric function and structure between patient groups and controls. At least two main areas of research, relating to patients with developmental language disorders (including dyslexia) and schizophrenia, have shown that effects are difficult to replicate across studies. This has been demonstrated for behavioral and brain measures (Cowell et al., in press; Hynd et al., 1995; Njiokiktjien, de Sonneville, & Vaal, 1994; Rumsey et al., 1996). This literature reflects a pattern of nonreproducibility similar to that seen in the normative studies and is further accentuated by the additional heterogeneity seen within and across patient samples. Recent data have shown not only that patients with certain neurodevelopmental disorders show aberrant patterns of neurocognitive asymmetry, but that their family members may have neuropsychological or neuroanatomical characteristics that fall somewhere between the clinical and normative profiles (Cannon et al., 1994; Leonard et al., 1993; Plante, 1991). Thus, factors such as family history of disorders associated with differences in interhemispheric relations and laterality may contribute further to the inability to replicate effects such as sex differences in studies of normative samples.

In many cases, ability to focus on only one or two independent variables is due to theoretical or practical issues that limit the scope of the data collection. However, at this stage in the field of interhemispheric relations, the potential effects of various individual factors have been identified. Now it is critical to move beyond the level of one- and two-factor designs in neuroimaging and function to examine a more complex constellation of variables that influence brain structure and function. We hypothesize, for example, that sex effects in the literature may have been diluted by previously unanalyzed interactions with factors such as age and hand preference, and vice versa.

In 1996 we attended a conference on sensorimotor integration and the corpus callosum. We presented independent findings, from data collected several years apart on different continents that reflected similar patterns of sex differences in the structure (Cowell et al., 1992; Cowell et al., in press) and function (Hugdahl, 1998, in press) of the corpus callosum, which varied as a function of age. These parallel findings suggested that if the data were examined in a certain way, reproducible trends could be shown in measures believed by some to be "too variable." This approach formed the basis for this study's collaboration and provided the rationale for the preliminary analysis described in this article.

We will address some of the methodological approaches that may help researchers perceive systematic variation, rather than nonreproducibility, in their data. These issues will be highlighted through the analysis of dichotic listening data that are part of an ongoing collaboration to study the development, organization, and disorders of laterality and interhemispheric relations across the human life span. We present these findings as a means to demonstrate multidimensional approaches to design, analysis, and interpretation.

METHOD

The data presented in this article are from a normative study of brain and behavior across the life span in healthy men and women. Participants were 57 healthy male ($n=25$) and female ($n=32$) volunteers ranging in age from 20 to 72 years. Each participant was administered a background interview to screen for physical and mental illnesses that could affect brain function. The dichotic listening test was administered as part of a larger neurocognitive battery of tasks designed to be sensitive to individual differences related to factors such as sex and age. A subset of these participants also received brain scans using structural magnetic resonance imaging techniques. The neuroanatomical and full behavioral databases are not included in this analysis.

The dichotic stimuli used in this study consisted of the six stop consonants (/b/, /d/, /g/, /p/, /t/, and /k/) paired with the vowel /a/ to form six consonant–vowel (CV) syllables (/ba/, /da/, /ga/, /pa/, /ta/, and /ka/). The syllables were paired with each other in all possible combinations, thus creating 36 different syllable pairs. The homonymic pairs (/ba/-/ba/, etc.) were included as a perceptual control that the participants did perceive the various stimuli. They were not included in the statistical analyses. The 36 dichotic pairs were recorded three times on compact disc (CD) with three different randomizations. There were 36 trials for each attentional instruction. Thus, a maximum correct score was 30 (excluding the 6 homonyms). The syllables were read by a male voice, with intonation and intensity held constant. The syllables were digitized (22,000-Hz sampling frequency per channel) before computerized editing and temporal alignment of stimulus onset. The alignment of the CV pairs across channels was done by displaying each CV pair on a computer screen, simultaneously listening to the CV pairs, and aligning them for consonant onset as well as overall duration by editing in the vowel segment. The computer editing was done with the PC-based sound-editing program SoundSwell. The syllables had a duration of approximately 400 msec, with 4-sec intervals. Each syllable pair was digitally recorded on a digital audiotape recorder and stored as a separate file on a PC. The files were then etched onto a CD connected to the PC and were later played to the participants from a standard CD player through headphones. The stimuli, as played through the experimental equipment, were tested to ensure equivalent peak loudness for each syllable in each ear.

The participants were told that they would be presented with a list of CV syllables. Their task was to answer with the syllable they heard on each trial. Thus, one response for each trial was emphasized. If they were able to identify both syllables on a trial, they were nevertheless told to report only the one they heard "most clearly." In a second condition, the participants were instructed to pay attention only to the right ear (forced-right [FR] condition) and to report only from that ear. In a third condition, they were instructed to pay attention only to the left ear (forced-left [FL] condition) and to report only from that ear. The order of presentation of the FR and FL conditions was counterbalanced across the participants.

RESULTS

The findings of these analyses are not presented as definitive results; rather, they are intended to provide a vehicle for exploring the multidimensional nature of functional laterality and interhemispheric function. Ideally, the data would have been analyzed simultaneously for numerous variables known to affect the behavioral and neurobiological manifestations of laterality and interhemispheric relations. Such an analysis was precluded by the relatively small size and demographics of our sample. Therefore, we present semi-independent analyses to show how sex, age, handedness, and family history of developmental language and learning disorder including dyslexia (FLD) affect dichotic listening performance.

Differences With Sex, Handedness, and FLD: Comparisons of Means

Table 1 shows the asymmetry coefficients [(RE – LE)/(RE + LE)] for right ear (RE) and left ear (LE) responses (Davidson & Hugdahl, 1996) for the three attention conditions, nonforced (NF), FL, and FR. For purposes of evaluating the relative contribution of each ear, absolute measures of right- and left-ear performance are shown in Table 2 for the same subgroups of participants and test conditions shown in Table 1.

The relative asymmetry data shown in Table 1 for the NF condition reflect trends observed in the literature (for overviews, see Bryden, 1988; Hugdahl, 1995; Lake & Bryden, 1976). Specifically, asymmetry coefficients are positive, indicating an overall superior performance from the right ear. The REA was stronger for men than for women and stronger for right-handers than for left-handers of both sexes.

If one looks across the three attention conditions, further trends can be observed. The rightward bias in the asymmetry coefficients is enhanced in the FR condition for all groups except the subgroup of left-handed and ambidextrous women, in which the mean stayed roughly the same in the NF and forced conditions. In contrast, there was an attenuation of the rightward bias in the asymmetry coefficients in the FL con-

TABLE 1
Means and Standard Errors of Dichotic Listening Asymmetry Scores for the Total Sample and Various Subgroups of Participants

Group	*n*	*NF*	*FL*	*FR*
All	57	.12 ± .03	.06 ± .04	.21 ± .04
Women	32	.08 ± .04	.04 ± .05	.15 ± .05
Right-handed women	26	.10 ± .04	.07 ± .05	.18 ± .06
Left-handed and ambidextrous women	6	.02 ± .11	–.09 ± .11	.01 ± .05
Right-handed women (no FLD)	18	.01 ± .05	–.01 ± .07	.14 ± .08
Men	25	.17 ± .05	.10 ± .06	.30 ± .05
Right-handed men	22	.20 ± .05	.13 ± .06	.32 ± .05
Left-handed and ambidextrous men	3	.01 ± .25	–.10 ± .19	.13 ± .26
Right-handed men (no FLD)	17	.20 ± .07	.13 ± .07	.32 ± .06

Note. In some cases, standard errors will underestimate significance of within-subject comparisons done across the attention conditions. The asymmetry coefficients were calculated according to the following formula: [(RE – LE) / (RE + LE)]. NF = nonforced attention condition; FL = forced-left attention condition; FR = forced-right attention condition; FLD = family history of developmental language and learning disorder including dyslexia; RE = right ear; LE = left ear.

TABLE 2
Means and Standard Errors of Absolute Dichotic Listening Performance for the Total Sample and Various Subgroups of Participants

		NF		*FL*		*FR*	
Group	*n*	*Right Ear*	*Left Ear*	*Right Ear*	*Left Ear*	*Right Ear*	*Left Ear*
All	57	11.5 ± 0.4	8.8 ± 0.3	10.9 ± 0.4	9.6 ± 0.4	13.0 ± 0.5	8.3 ± 0.4
Women	32	11.1 ± 0.5	9.3 ± 0.4	11.0 ± 0.6	10.2 ± 0.6	12.3 ± 0.6	9.1 ± 0.5
RH women	26	11.3 ± 0.6	9.2 ± 0.5	11.5 ± 0.6	10.0 ± 0.7	12.7 ± 0.7	8.8 ± 0.6
LHA women	6	10.2 ± 1.4	9.7 ± 1.0	9.0 ± 1.0	11.0 ± 1.4	10.8 ± 0.7	10.5 ± 0.7
RH women (no FLD)	18	11.4 ± 0.7	9.2 ± 0.6	10.6 ± 0.7	10.9 ± 0.9	12.2 ± 1.0	9.1 ± 0.8
Men	25	11.9 ± 0.7	8.2 ± 0.5	10.8 ± 0.7	8.8 ± 0.6	13.9 ± 0.9	7.2 ± 0.5
RH men	22	12.3 ± 0.7	8.2 ± 0.6	11.1 ± 0.7	8.7 ± 0.7	14.2 ± 1.0	6.9 ± 0.5
LHA men	3	9.0 ± 2.6	8.3 ± 1.8	8.7 ± 2.7	10.0 ± 1.2	9.3 ± 2.7	8.7 ± 2.7
RH men (no FLD)	17	12.6 ± 0.8	8.2 ± 0.7	11.6 ± 0.7	9.1 ± 0.9	14.5 ± 1.0	7.2 ± 0.6

Note. In some cases, standard errors will underestimate significance of within-subject comparisons done across the attention conditions. NF = nonforced attention condition; FL = forced-left attention condition; FR = forced-right attention condition; RH = right-handed; LHA = left-handed and/or ambidextrous; FLD = family history of developmental language and learning disorder including dyslexia.

dition for all groups. The left-handed and ambidextrous participants, in both the male and female groups, showed near symmetry in the NF and FR conditions and obtained leftward-biased asymmetry coefficients in the FL condition.

An analysis of variance (ANOVA), with *sex* as a grouping factor and attention condition as a repeated measure, was performed using asymmetry scores for right-handed men (n = 17; mean age = 38.2 years, SE = 3.0) and women (n = 18; mean age = 46.6 years, SE = 3.2) with no FLD. A significant sex effect was found, $F(1, 33) = 4.22, p < .05$, indicating that the REA was greater for men than for women across all test conditions. This effect was strongest in the FR condition, $F(1, 33) = 3.33, p < .08$ and weakest in the NF condition (*ns*). The effect of attention condition was also significant, $F(2, 66) = 4.82, p < .05$, indicating that for both sexes, compared to the NF condition, there was a decrease in the rightward-biased asymmetry coefficient in the FL condition and an increase in the rightward-biased asymmetry coefficient in the FR condition. This resulted in a significant difference between the FR and FL conditions, paired $t(34) = 3.06, p < .01$.

When the same analysis was applied to the right-handers including participants with FLD (n = 48) and to the entire sample of participants (N = 57), the levels of statistical significance for sex effects were decreased to $p < .10$, despite increased sample sizes. This indicated a sensitivity of sex differences in asymmetry coefficients to direction of handedness and FLD. Attention condition effects remained significant at $p < .01$, which reflected robusticity of the relative effects of the attention conditions with respect to handedness and FLD.

Examination of the data in Table 2 shows the sources of variation in the asymmetry coefficients with respect to each ear. For example, several phenomena contributed to the significant sex difference in asymmetry observed in the FR condition. In right-handed women without FLD (n = 18), the difference in REA seen between the NF and FR conditions was due to the combined effects of a slight increase in number of correct right-ear responses (+0.8) and virtually no change in number of correct left-ear responses (–0.1). This resulted in a net increase of 0.7 total correct responses. In right-handed men without FLD (n = 17), there was a more notable increase in REA when switching from the NF to the FR conditions; this difference was due to an increase in correct right-ear responses (+1.9) and a decrease in left-ear responses (–1.0), resulting in a net increase of 0.9 total correct responses. Thus, although the total number of correct responses was similar for men and women in both NF and FR conditions, the contributions of each ear to the NF–FR difference in asymmetry coefficients appear subtly different between the sexes.

Differences With Sex, Handedness, and FLD: Comparisons of Correlations

Asymmetry scores for the three attention conditions were correlated for the whole group of right-handers without FLD (n = 35) and separately for men and women. For the whole group, degree of asymmetry in the baseline NF condition was correlated with degree of asymmetry in the FR condition, $r(33) = .42, p < .05$. Asymmetry scores for the FR and FL conditions were correlated with each other, $r(33)= .37, p < .05$. For men, only the FR–FL correlation remained significant, $r(15) = .5, p < .05$. For women, only the NF–FR correlation remained significant, $r(16)= .51, p<.05$.

With these effects serving as the baseline, further analyses were conducted to investigate the effects of age on dichotic listening performance using right-handed men and women with no FLD.

Differences as a Function of Sex, Age, and Test Condition

An ANOVA with *sex* as a grouping factor, *age* as a covariate, and *attention condition* as a repeated measure was performed for the 35 participants (17 men, 18 women) used in the analyses discussed previously. The right-handed women without FLD (age range 21–64, mean age = 46.6 ± 3.3 years) were marginally older than the right-handed men without FLD (age range 22–63, mean age = 38.2 ± 3.0 years), $t(33) = 1.86, p < .10$. This analysis allowed us to control for, and examine the effects of, age on both the total number of correct responses and the asymmetry scores.

For total correct responses, there were no significant main effects related to age or sex, nor were there any interactions of these factors with attention condition.

For the asymmetry coefficients, there were no significant effects of sex, age, or Sex × Age across the three attentional conditions. As seen in the analyses of sex effects discussed previously, attention condition remained significant, $F(2, 62) = 7.43, p < .01$. Condition also interacted significantly with sex, $F(2, 62) = 4.86, p < .05$, age, $F(2, 62) = 4.20, p < .05$, and Sex × Age, $F(2, 62) = 4.63, p < .05$, suggesting that all three factors contributed to variation in asymmetry scores. Further analyses were conducted to examine the relative contributions of sex and age to each attention condition.

For the NF condition, there was a significant interaction of Sex × Age, $F(1, 31) = 4.03, p < .06$. In men, NF asymmetry was positively correlated with age ($r = .34$, *ns*), whereas in women, NF asymmetry was negatively correlated with age ($r = –.34$, *ns*). Taken together, these moderate, although nonsignificant correlations, indicated that older men have a greater REA than younger men, but that older women have a lower REA than younger women. This relation is depicted in Figure 1.

For the FR condition, there was a significant age effect, $F(1, 31) = 4.27, p < .05$. In both men and women, FR asymmetry scores were negatively correlated with age, $r(33) = –.42, p < .05$, indicating that younger participants had greater REAs in the FR condition than older participants did. This relation is depicted in Figure 2.

For the FL condition, sex was significant, $F(1, 31) = 3.8, p < .06$, indicating that male–female differences observed in the previous section were robust to the effects of age. There was also a nonsignificant trend for an interaction between sex

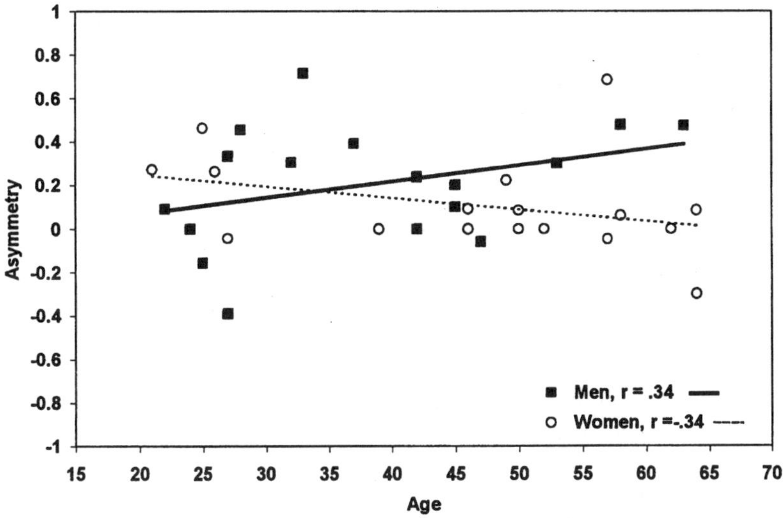

FIGURE 1 Sex × Age effects for the nonforced condition. Asymmetry scores for men (squares and bold regression line) as a function of age are compared with asymmetry scores for women (circles and light regression line).

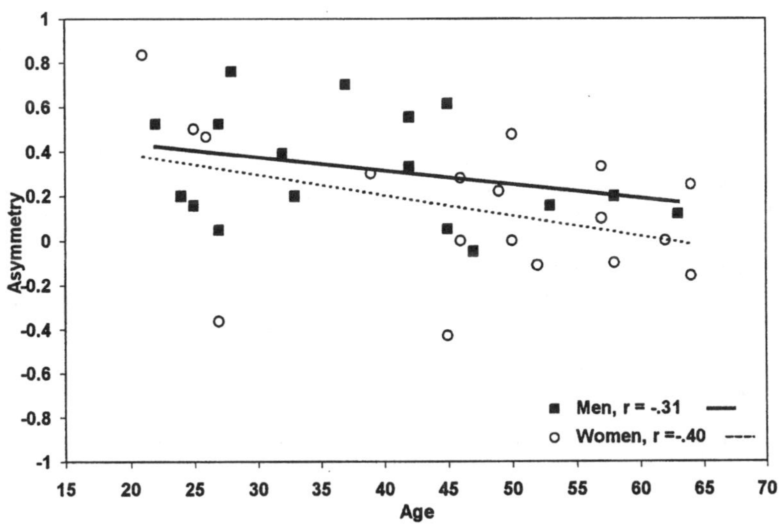

FIGURE 2 Age effects for the forced-right condition. Asymmetry scores for men (squares and bold regression line) as a function of age are compared with asymmetry scores for women (circles and light regression line).

and age in the FL condition, $F(1, 31) = 2.25, p < .15$. Further investigation of this trend revealed a marginally significant correlation between age and asymmetry coefficients in the FL condition in women, $r(16) = .44, p < .07$, but not in men. The positive correlation in women reflects more leftward asymmetry scores in younger women compared to older women. This relation is depicted in Figure 3.

DISCUSSION

The discussion focuses on two aspects of the findings presented previously. We will comment on the multiple factors that influence ear asymmetries in dichotic listening performance and that contribute to the presence of individual differences. In addition, we will address how the forced-attention conditions are ideal for highlighting individual differences, because they allow one to examine multiple neurocognitive dimensions of interhemispheric and lateralized function.

In an ideal study there would be sufficient sample sizes to accommodate statistical analyses for multiple factors previously shown to affect neurobehavioral asymmetries and interhemispheric relations. In this study's analysis, we had insufficient numbers of left-handers and participants with FLD to simultaneously analyze for sex, age, handedness, FLD, and their interactions. However, through a

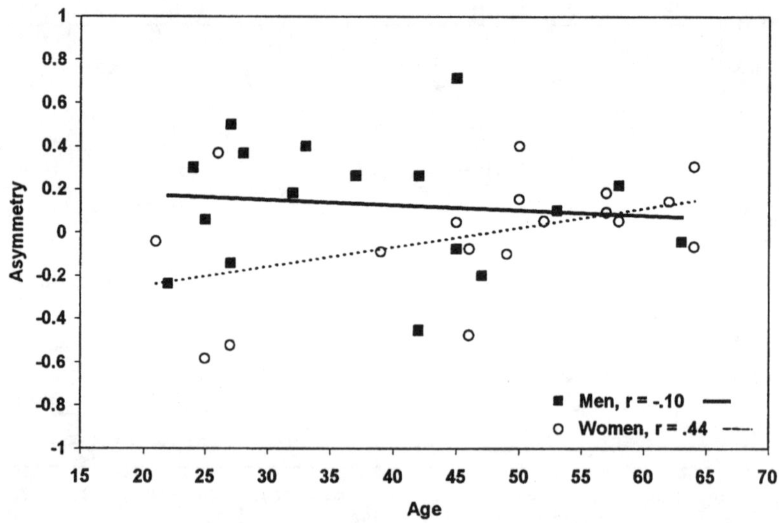

FIGURE 3 Sex effects and Sex × Age effects for the forced-left condition. Asymmetry scores for men (squares and bold regression line) as a function of age are compared with asymmetry scores for women (circles and light regression line).

combination of semi-independent analyses, we have shown that all of these factors seem to affect the nature of the REA in the NF and forced-attention conditions. This may account for why it has been so difficult to replicate findings in the study of dichotic listening and related neuroanatomical structures such as the corpus callosum. Reports in the literature vary with respect to the age ranges of their participants. Some are performed on university undergraduates (Davidson & Hugdahl, 1996; Lake & Bryden, 1976), whereas others are likely to span portions of the age range that we have shown to be sensitive to interactive effects with sex (Altemus, Wexler, & Boulis, 1989; Dawe & Corballis, 1986). In light of findings that relatives of individuals with developmental language disorders had atypical inter- and intrahemispheric asymmetries (Leonard et al., 1993; Plante, 1991), and that some of these neuroanatomical features were correlated with phonological test scores (Leonard et al., 1993), it is possible that the presence of participants with FLD may attenuate the REA in studies in which participants are not specifically screened for this factor.

For the reasons mentioned previously, behavioral measures of laterality may sometimes provide conflicting results across studies, not because the measures lack validity, but because they are affected by genetic, hormonal, or developmental factors that interact with the expression of the asymmetry. In addition, as suggested by Hugdahl (1995), auditory laterality is not mediated by a single mechanism but is influenced both by automatic perceptual processes and by more consciously controlled cognitive processes, such as shifting of attention. Therefore, factors such as sex, age, handedness, and FLD may contribute to individual differences in dichotic listening at multiple behaviorocognitive levels. This study examined group differences both across and within three testing conditions to provide insight into "stimulus-driven" perceptual processing asymmetries as well as higher order cognitive capacities that contributed to the observed laterality scores, particularly in forced-attention conditions.

Greater REA in men across the three conditions suggests a pervasive perceptual sex difference regardless of attentional focus or shift. Greater asymmetries in dichotic listening may be linked to greater asymmetries in cortical regions involved in auditory processing (Kulynych, Vladar, Jones, & Weinberger, 1994). The fact that this REA appears stronger in older men compared to younger men in this study (Figure 1) may be due to numerous changes in regional cortical and callosal neuroanatomy or function with age that are discussed later. However, given the sensitivity of the REA in this study to direction of handedness, particularly in men (see Table 1), it is possible that differences in our older and younger male groups may also have been related to differences in degree of right-handedness, a factor shown to affect both the anatomy of the callosal isthmus (Cowell et al., 1993; Witelson, 1989) and the size of related cortical structures (Witelson & Kigar, 1992).

Another cross-condition difference of note was the pattern of correlation between asymmetry scores in men and women in the NF, FR, and FL tasks. In men, the correlation between FR and FL asymmetry was stronger than the relations between NF asymmetry scores and those from either forced-attention condition. In women, only the correlation between the NF and FR asymmetries was significant. These results provide support for the view that men and women use different cognitive mechanisms in the focused-attention conditions that interact in unique ways with the basic underlying difference in lateralized perceptual processing. One possible explanation for these results is that in men, the degree of asymmetry was affected by the instruction to focus attention, and that in both right- and left-focused conditions, it was the ability to focus rather than underlying perceptual asymmetry that determined laterality scores. In women, it appears that in the FR condition, the laterality scores varied as a function of the underlying perceptual asymmetry in the NF condition. Therefore, it may only be in the FL condition that ability to focus attention contributes to asymmetry scores. Further neuropsychological analysis of dichotic listening scores with other measures of perceptual asymmetry and attentional abilities would be needed to confirm this interpretation.

Regardless of which specific components contributed to the differences in intercorrelation between asymmetry scores described previously, these patterns suggest that any aspect of dichotic listening performance, even age-related decreases in REA in the FR condition that appeared similar in men and women, may be subserved by different underlying cognitive mechanisms. The finding that there are sex differences within NF and FL conditions provides further support for the view that different neurocognitive mechanisms are recruited in men and women even when they are ostensibly performing the same dichotic listening task.

Examination of the age-related sex differences in asymmetry scores from the NF condition, in conjunction with information on the age-related sex differences in the brain, sheds light on possible neurobehavioral differences in the source of the REA in men and women. Davidson and Hugdahl (1996) showed that multiple cortical regions were involved in even the basic NF condition in which a larger REA was associated with patterns of greater left temporoparietal and right prefrontal electroencephalogram activation. Frontal and temporal cortical volumes and anterior callosal widths (Cowell et al., 1992; Cowell et al., 1994) have been shown to begin decreasing in men some time between the third and fifth decades of life. In women, age-related decreases in volume are more prevalent in the parieto-occipital cortex (Murphy et al., 1996) and are combined with increases in anterior callosal measures between the third and fifth decades of life (Aboitiz et al., 1996; Cowell et al., 1992). Thus, it is possible that the increase in REA in men and the decrease in REA in women with advancing age in the NF condition (Figure 1) were associated with regional sex differences in cortical aging. Moreover, it is possible that decreases in callosal size with age in men are related to greater separation of the hemispheres and increased REA. In contrast, increases during midlife in regional corpus callosum size in women may lead to less separation of the hemispheres and decreases in REA. The issue of callosum size and behavioral asymmetry has been discussed by Clarke and Zaidel (1994), although not with respect to sex differences in aging.

In a situation in which there is a strong perceptual asymmetry in auditory processing (i.e., a strong REA), the dichotic nature of the presentation of the CV syllables stimuli will automatically favor the right-ear input because of both the anatomy of the auditory pathways (Brodal, 1981) and a left-hemisphere dominance for phonological processing (Fitch, Miller, & Tallal, 1997). Therefore, the FL condition represents a conflict between automatic, stimulus-driven processing (which favors the right ear) and controlled, instruction-driven processing (which, in this case, forces use of the left ear). Under such conditions, the participant is forced to deal with two opposing lateralized tendencies simultaneously, which requires allocation of additional information processing resources. Achieving an actual LEA in this situation (i.e., a negative asymmetry score) seemed to be achievable mainly by the left-handers and ambidexters in this study, perhaps because they had less of a baseline REA to contend with compared to the right-handers (Table 1).

Degree of asymmetry in the NF condition did not correlate with degree of asymmetry in the FL condition in right-handers. Therefore, both the attenuation in asymmetry scores that was observed in the FL condition and the sex differences in these scores must be attributed in large part to differences in attention-focusing mechanisms rather than to baseline perceptual asymmetries. Table 2 shows that, whereas men modulated the relative number of right- and left-ear responses to produce a lower REA in the FL condition, women actually increased the total number of correct responses through an increased number of left-ear responses. This ability to achieve leftward asymmetry was achieved more successfully by the younger women than the older women in the group (Figure 3). It is possible that this group of younger women had greater cognitive flexibility or executive attentional capacity to modulate and override response tendencies driven by the sensory stimulus than older women did. If this ability to achieve a symmetric or leftward asymmetry in the FL condition is related to the integrity of the corpus callosum, this is difficult to resolve with the reports that subregions of this structure (and cytoarchitectural correlates) increase in size in women through the fifth decade of life (Aboitiz et al., 1996; Cowell et al., 1992). However, such hypotheses are based on lines of thinking that involve cross-study integration of results from independent samples of participants. Analysis of data samples with both anatomical and behavioral measurements will be necessary to address these questions further.

This discussion not only has relevance to behavioral studies in humans, but also has applications to the study of the organization, development, and plasticity of laterality and interhemispheric relations in general. In this article and in previous work by Hugdahl and colleagues (Hugdahl, 1998, in press; Reinvang, Bakke, Hugdahl, Karlsen, & Sundet, 1994), the forced-attention conditions have been useful in highlighting individual differences in performance associated with development, aging, and clinical conditions. By challenging the neurobehavioral system to perform under conditions that modulate sensory input, one can create a paradigm that highlights individual differences by either complementing or opposing the naturally occurring pattern. A similar type of approach was used in rats to investigate environmentally induced changes in laterality of the neurobehavioral systems involved in spatial navigation (Cowell, Waters, & Denenberg, 1997). Rats receiving a chronic, low-grade environmental stressor for the first 21 days of life showed similar performance to controls in Morris maze performance. However, differences between these groups of animals were found when they were challenged by having to wear either a right or a left eye patch during the task. That study, together with this study's preliminary findings, support the general notion that group differences in laterality can be subtle or masked in naturally occurring behavior. Restrictions in sensory input (as in the rodent study) or attentional shift (as in the human study) may be highly effective in studying variation in the functional organization of these systems.

These analyses have provided some insight into why certain behavioral manifestations of interhemispheric function, in this case dichotic listening performance, are so varied from study to study. Indeed, one early impetus for this collaboration was to investigate further a Sex × Age interaction effect in left-ear responses in the FL condition (Hugdahl, in press) that mirrored trends seen in the regional anatomical size of the anterior corpus callosum (Cowell et al., 1992). In this analysis, we were unable to replicate the former effect, and we believe this may be due to a number of factors. In this study, there were insufficient participants in the older age range, which may have restricted variability, contributing to the age effects previously observed by Hugdahl (in press). This confirms the importance of matching samples for age when comparing effects on dichotic listening performance. We have also noted that overall performance for total right- and left-ear responses was better in Hugdahl's (in press) sample across all attention conditions. Thus, certain aspects of laterality and interhemispheric function may only be observed in participants performing at or above a certain baseline level.

The results of this study suggest that even within a healthy, normative sample of human participants, individuals vary not only in their underlying perceptual asymmetries for auditory input, but also in the manner in which such asymmetries interact with other higher order cognitive functions involved in interhemispheric relations. This observation has strong implications for the study of how perceptual asymmetries relate to language organization, development, and disorder. For example, sex differences both in baseline laterality scores and in asymmetry in the forced-attention conditions in this task of auditory perception may account in part for reports showing that women have a greater degree of bilateral cortical activity than men when performing verbal rhyming and lexical tasks (Shaywitz et al., 1995; Wood, Flowers, & Naylor, 1991). In particular, the lower REA in the NF condition in all right-handed women compared to men and the greater leftward attenuation of asymmetry seen in the younger women may underlie the effects seen in studies of higher order language functions.

Using additional brain and behavioral measures that are part of the larger database, we will investigate other factors that may contribute to individual differences in dichotic listening performance, such as hormonal status (Altemus et al., 1989; Rode, Wagner, & Gunturkun, 1995; Sanders & Wenmoth, 1998; Weekes & Zaidel, 1996; also see Hugdahl, 1999) and direction and degree of motor asymmetries, including handedness (Cowell et al., 1993; Geffen, Jones, & Geffen, 1994) and the microacoustic properties of the CV syllables (for overviews, see Beeman & Chiarello, 1998; Bryden & Bulman-Fleming, 1994; Ivry & Lebby, 1998). We also plan to apply the approach used in this study to analyze regional anatomical subfields of the corpus callosum and related outlying cortical volumes in individuals with dyslexia. Such an approach may be exemplified with recent findings from Hugdahl's laboratory, where shape of the body and isthmus of the corpus callosum was found to be different in children with dyslexia compared to controls. Because the neural connections from right and left superior temporal gyri project through this region (Lamantia & Rakic, 1990; Pandya & Seltzer, 1986; Pandya, Karol, & Heilbronn, 1971), anatomical differences may be related to impaired auditory phonological processing in dyslexia. This will be tested with the dichotic listening CV syllables technique by correlating regional callosal size with various performance measures.

ACKNOWLEDGMENTS

This project was funded by Grant 18916 from the Royal Society Research to Patricia Cowell and from Grant 115353/320 from the Norwegian Research Council to Kenneth Hugdahl.

We thank R. A. Varley for helpful advice on the behavioral testing, and P. Martland for testing the equipment.

REFERENCES

Aboitiz, F., Rodriguez, E., Olivares, R., & Zaidel, E. (1996). Age-related changes in fibre composition of the human corpus callosum: Sex differences. *NeuroReport, 7,* 1761–1764.

Altemus, M., Wexler, B., & Boulis, N. (1989). Changes in perceptual asymmetry with the menstrual cycle. *Neuropsychologia, 27,* 233–240.

Beeman, M. J., & Chiarello, C. (1998). Complementary right- and left-hemisphere language comprehension. *Current Directions in Psychological Science, 7,* 2–8.

Bishop, K. M., & Wahlsten, D. (1997). Sex differences in the human corpus callosum: Myth or reality? *Neuroscience and Biobehavioral Reviews, 21,* 581–601.

Brodal, A. (Ed.). (1981). *Neurological anatomy in relation to clinical medicine* (3rd ed.). New York: Oxford University Press.

Bryden, M. P. (1988). Dichotic studies of the lateralization of affect in normal subjects. In K. Hugdahl (Ed.), *Handbook of dichotic listening: Theory, methods, and research* (pp. 359–374). Chichester, England: Wiley.

Bryden, M. P., & Bulman-Fleming, M. B. (1994). Laterality effects in normal subjects: Evidence for interhemispheric interactions. *Behavioural Brain Research, 64,* 119–129.

Cannon, T. D., Eyler Zorilla, L., Shtasel, D. L., Gur, R. E., Gur, R. C., Marco, E. J., Moberg, P., & Price, R. A. (1994). Neuropsychological functioning in siblings discordant for schizophrenia and healthy volunteers. *Archives of General Psychiatry, 51,* 651–661.

Clarke, J. M., & Zaidel, E. (1994). Anatomical–behavioral relationships: Corpus callosum morphometry and hemispheric specialization. *Behavioral Brain Research, 64,* 185–202.

Cowell, P. E., Allen, L. S., Zalatimo, N. S., & Denenberg, V. H. (1992). A developmental study of sex and age interactions in the human corpus callosum. *Developmental Brain Research, 66,* 187–192.

Cowell, P. E., Denenberg, V., Boehm, G., Kertesz, A., & Nasrallah, H. (in press). Using the corpus callosum as an effective anatomical probe in the study of schizophrenia. In E. Zaidel & M. Iacoboni (Eds.), *The parallel brain: The cognitive neuroscience of the corpus callosum.* Cambridge, MA: MIT Press.

Cowell, P. E., Kertesz, A., & Denenberg, V. H. (1993). Multiple dimensions of handedness and the human corpus callosum. *Neurology, 43,* 2353–2357.

Cowell, P. E., Turetsky, B. I., Gur, R. C., Shtasel, D. L., Grossman, R. I., & Gur, R. E. (1994). Sex differences in aging of the human frontal and temporal lobes. *Journal of Neuroscience, 14,* 4748–4755.

Cowell, P. E., Waters, N. S., & Denenberg, V. H. (1997). Effects of early environment on the development of functional laterality in Morris maze performance. *Laterality, 2,* 221–232.

Davidson, R. J., & Hugdahl, K. (1996). Baseline asymmetries in brain electrical activity predict dichotic listening performance. *Neuropsychology, 10,* 241–246.

Dawe, S., & Corballis, M. (1986). The influence of gender, handedness and head-turn on auditory asymmetries. *Neuropsychologia, 24,* 857–862.

Fitch, R. H., Miller, S., & Tallal, P. (1997). Neurobiology of speech perception [Annual review]. *Neuroscience, 20,* 331–353.

Geffen, G. M., Jones, D. L., & Geffen, L. B. (1994). Interhemispheric control of manual motor activity. *Behavioural Brain Research, 64,* 131–140.

Habib, M., Gayraud, D., Oliva, A., Regis, J., Salamon, G., & Khalil, R. (1991). Effects of handedness and sex on the morphology of the corpus callosum: A study with brain magnetic resonance imaging. *Brain and Cognition, 16,* 41–61.

Hiscock, M., Inch, R., Jacek, C., Hiscock-Kalil, C., & Kalil, K. M. (1994). Is there a sex difference in human laterality? I. An exhaustive survey of auditory laterality studies from six neuropsychology journals. *Journal of Clinical and Experimental Neuropsychology, 16,* 423–435.

Hugdahl, K. (1995). Dichotic listening: Probing temporal lobe functional integrity. In R. J. Davidson & K. Hugdahl (Eds.), *Brain asymmetry* (pp. 123–156). Cambridge, MA: MIT Press.

Hugdahl, K. (1998). The corpus callosum: More than a “passive” corpus [Commentary]. *Behavioral and Brain Sciences, 21,* 335.

Hugdahl, K. (1999). Brain lateralization: Dichotic listening studies. In G. Adelman & B. H. Smith (Eds.), *Elsevier’s encyclopedia of neuroscience* (2nd enlarged ed., pp. 276–279). Amsterdam: Elsevier.

Hugdahl, K. (in press). Attentional modulation of interhemispheric transfer of auditory information: A “two-channel threshold” model. In E. Zaidel & M. Iacoboni (Eds.), *The parallel brain: The cognitive neuroscience of the corpus callosum.* Cambridge, MA: MIT Press.

Hynd, G. W., Hall, J., Novey, E. S., Eliopulos, D., Black, K., Gonzalez, J. J., Edmonds, J. E., Riccio, C., & Cohen, M. (1995). Dyslexia and corpus callosum morphology. *Archives of Neurology, 52,* 32–38.

Ivry, R., & Lebby, P. C. (1998). The neurology of consonant perception: Specialized module or distributed processors? In M. Beeman & C. Chiarello (Eds.), *Right hemisphere language comprehen-*

sion perspectives from cognitive neuroscience (pp. 3–25). Mahwah, NJ: Lawrence Erlbaum Associates, Inc.

Kulynych, J. J., Vladar, K., Jones, D. W., & Weinberger, D. R. (1994). Gender differences in the normal lateralization of the supratemporal cortex: MRI surface-rendering morphometry of Heschl's hyrus and the planum temporale. *Cerebral Cortex, 4,* 107–118.

Lake, D. A., & Bryden, M. P. (1976). Handedness and sex differences in hemispheric asymmetry. *Brain and Language, 3,* 266–282.

Lamantia, A. S., & Rakic, P. (1990). Cytological and quantitative characteristics of four cerebral commissures in the rhesus monkey. *Journal of Comparative Neurology, 291,* 520–537.

Leonard, C. M., Voeller, K. K. S., Lombardino, L. J., Morris, M. K., Hynd, G. W., Alexander, A. W., Andersen, H. G., Garotalakis, M., Honeyman, J. C., Mao, J., Agee, F., & Staab, E. V. (1993). Anomalous cerebral structure in dyslexia revealed with magnetic resonance imaging. *Archives of Neurology, 50,* 461–469.

McKeever, W. F. (1986). Tachistoscopic methods in neuropsychology. In J. Hannay (Ed.), *Experimental techniques in human neuropsychology* (pp. 167–211). New York: Oxford University Press.

Murphy, D. G. M., DeCarli, C., McIntosh, A. R., Daly, E., Mentis, M. J., Pietrini, P., Szczepanik, J., Schapiro, M. B., Grady, C. L., Horwitz, B., & Rapoport, S. I. (1996). Sex differences in human brain morphometry and metabolism: An in vivo quantitative magnetic resonance imaging and positron emission tomography study of the effect of aging. *Archives of General Psychiatry, 53,* 585–594.

Njiokiktjien, C., de Sonneville, L., & Vaal, J. (1994). Callosal size in children with learning disabilities. *Behavioural Brain Research, 64,* 213–218.

Pandya, D. N., Karol, E. A., & Heilbronn, D. (1971). The topographical distribution of interhemispheric projections in the corpus callosum of the rhesus monkey. *Brain Research, 32,* 31–43.

Pandya, D., & Seltzer, B. (1986). The topography of commissural fibers. In F. Lepore, M. Ptito, & H. Jaspar (Eds.), *Two hemispheres—one brain: Functions of the corpus callosum* (pp. 47–73). New York: Alan Liss.

Plante, E. (1991). MRI findings in the parents and siblings of specifically language-impaired boys. *Brain and Language, 41,* 67–80.

Rauch, R. A., & Jinkins, J. R. (1994). Analysis of cross-sectional area measurements of the corpus callosum adjusted for brain size in male and female subjects from childhood to adulthood. *Behavioural Brain Research, 64,* 65–78.

Reinvang, I., Bakke, S. J., Hugdahl, K., Karlsen, N. R., & Sundet, K. (1994). Dichotic listening performance in relation to callosal area on the MRI scan. *Neuropsychology, 8,* 445–450.

Rode, C., Wagner, M., & Gunturkun, O. (1995). Menstrual cycle affects functional cerebral asymmetries. *Neuropsychologia, 33,* 855–865.

Rumsey, J. M., Casanova, M., Mannheim, G. B., Patronas, N., DeVaughn, N., Hamburger, S. D., & Aquino, T. (1996). Corpus callosum morphology, as measured with MRI, in dyslexic men. *Biological Psychiatry, 39,* 769–775.

Sanders, G., & Wenmoth, D. (1998). Verbal and music dichotic listening tasks reveal variations in functional cerebral asymmetry across the menstrual cycle that are phase and task dependent. *Neuropsychologia, 36,* 869–874.

Shaywitz, B. A., Shaywitz, S. E., Pugh, K. R., Constable, R. T., Skudlarski, P., Fulbright, R. K., Bronen, R. A., Fletcher, J. M., Shankweiler, D. P., Katz, L., & Gore, J. C. (1995). Sex differences in the functional organization of the brain for language. *Nature, 373,* 607–609.

Weekes, N. Y., & Zaidel, E. (1996). The effects of procedural variations on lateralized Stroop effects. *Brain and Cognition, 31,* 308–330.

Witelson, S. (1989). Hand and sex differences in the isthmus and genu of the human corpus callosum. *Brain, 112,* 799–835.

Witelson, S. F., & Kigar, D. L. (1992). Sylvian fissure morphology and asymmetry in men and women: Bilateral differences in relation to handedness in men. *Journal of Comparative Neurology, 323,* 326–340.

Wood, F. B., Flowers, L. D., & Naylor, C. E. (1991). Cerebral laterality in functional neuroimaging. In F. L. Kitterle (Ed.), *Cerebral laterality: Theory and research—the Toledo symposium* (pp. 103–115). Hillsdale, NJ: Lawrence Erlbaum Associates, Inc.

DEVELOPMENTAL NEUROPSYCHOLOGY, *18*(1), 113–137

Differential Effects of Aging on the Functions of the Corpus Callosum

Patricia A. Reuter-Lorenz
Department of Psychology
University of Michigan

Louise Stanczak
Department of Communication Disorders
Boston University

Several structural imaging studies have revealed atrophy in regions of the corpus callosum due to normal aging. We examined the performance of young and senior adults on 2 behavioral measures of interhemispheric interactions to test for possible functional consequences of callosal decline. In a simple reaction time task, the efficiency of sensorimotor transfer was assessed by comparing response times from conditions that required interhemispheric transfer (e.g., the left hand responding to a right visual field light) to those from conditions that did not require transfer (e.g., the left hand responding to a left visual field light). Older adults were selectively slower when interhemispheric transfer was required. In the second task, participants matched letters presented within the same visual field or in opposite visual fields. This task is thought to index attentional functions of the corpus callosum, in particular, callosal contributions to resource allocation (Banich, 1998). For more difficult tasks, older participants showed a performance advantage on bilateral conditions requiring transfer compared to unilateral conditions that did not require transfer. This advantage equaled or exceeded that observed in younger adults. Together these results suggest that age does not have uniform effects on callosal function. Whereas sensorimotor functions show age-related decline, attentional functions of the corpus callosum may be relatively preserved and assume a more prominent role in the aging brain.

The aging process has widespread effects on human performance and cognition. Whereas crystallized aspects of cognition, such as vocabulary and factual knowl-

Requests for reprints should be sent to Patricia A. Reuter-Lorenz, Department of Psychology, University of Michigan, 525 East University, Ann Arbor, MI 48109–1109. E-mail: parl@umich.edu

edge, tend to improve over the life span, performance on tasks that require the rapid organization and active manipulation of such information show age-related declines (for a review, see Craik & Salthouse, 1992). Aging effects are evident in a variety of long-term and working memory tasks (e.g., Park et al., 1996; Salthouse, 1992), and components of attentional functioning (e.g., Hartley, 1992) are also compromised with age. Even measures of simple perceptual speed show age-related slowing, and such effects become increasingly pronounced as task complexity increases (e.g., Salthouse, 1992, 1996). In the face of such ubiquitous effects, a major challenge in the cognitive neuroscience of aging is to determine which aspects of age-related cognitive decline are due to diffuse or global changes in neural functioning and which arise from more localized, focal deficiencies.

This article focuses on how aging affects interhemispheric interactions and the functions of the corpus callosum—the major white matter pathway interconnecting the left and right cerebral hemispheres. The corpus callosum plays an essential and fundamental role in the integration of lateralized sensory, cognitive, and motor operations. Therefore, a general decline in the neural functioning of the callosum could conceivably have widespread effects on human performance. On the other hand, neural aging may have specific and selective effects on the callosum, in which case we would expect specific and selective performance changes as well.

We advance the hypothesis that along with a decline in efficiency of specific callosal functions, aging is associated with the relative sparing and increased reliance on other callosal functions. The bulk of the work on aging and the callosum has used structural analysis techniques to determine that aging has small but reliable effects on the size of the corpus callosum. The handful of behavioral studies that have examined functional changes in interhemispheric interactions have found declines with age. However, these studies have focused on the sensorimotor functions of the corpus callosum. Relatively little is known about the effects of aging on the cognitive and attentional functions of the corpus callosum. We present some new behavioral evidence to indicate that age-related decline in callosal function is not uniform. We show that in older individuals, for whom simple sensorimotor function of the corpus callosum is compromised, the attentional functions of the callosum are relatively preserved and may even assume a more prominent role in cognitive processing. We consider these results in light of recent neuroimaging evidence, from our own lab and others, indicating greater bilateral activation in older adults on particular tasks. Although the function of such activation differences remains uncertain, this study's results point to possible compensatory processes that may serve to counteract some of the consequences of aging.

CALLOSAL STRUCTURE AND THE EFFECTS OF AGING

The corpus callosum is a midline brain structure that measures approximately 6 cm in length and contains between 200 and 350 million fibers in the average human adult. These interhemispheric connections are organized topographically, in that different parts of the cortex project through different regions of the corpus callosum (see de Lacoste, Kirkpatrick, & Ross, 1985; Pandya & Seltzer, 1986). Roughly speaking, the anterior third (genu) connects prefrontal cortices, and the middle third connects motor, somatosensory, and auditory cortices. The isthmus is immediately behind the midbody and interconnects temporal and parietal association areas, including those that subserve linguistic functions. The most posterior region (posterior fifth) of the callosum is the splenium, which carries visual fibers from the occipital cortex and from the temporal and parietal regions.

The fiber composition of the callosum varies as well, with thinner, less myelinated (slower-conducting) fibers achieving their greatest density in the anterior callosum and decreasing toward the posterior midbody. The larger, more heavily myelinated, and faster-conducting fibers have peak densities in the posterior pole of the splenium and the posterior midbody (e.g., Aboitiz, Scheibel, Fisher, & Zaidel, 1992a, 1992b). In addition, the corpus callosum contains many unmyelinated fibers, up to 31% in the monkey. This structural diversity mirrors considerable functional variation and leaves open the possibility that aging has nonuniform effects on the corpus callosum.

In vivo structural magnetic resonance imaging is the technique most frequently used to assess the effects of age on the size of the corpus callosum. Cross-sectional measurements of the corpus callosum are typically taken from midsagittal images. Although there is considerable variation in the techniques used to partition the callosum into subregions, the results from a number of studies using area or width measurements suggest a small but reliable reduction in the size of the corpus callosum after middle age (Hopper, Patel, Cann, Wilcox, & Schaeffer, 1994; Janowsky, Kaye, & Carper, 1996; for a review, see Thompson, Narr, Blanton, & Toga, in press). Several studies have reported aging effects that are specific to the most anterior regions of the corpus callosum (Allen, Richey, Chai, & Gorski, 1991; Hayakawa et al., 1989; Parashos, Wilkinson, & Coffey, 1995; Salat, Ward, Kaye, & Janowsky, 1997; Weis, Jellinger, & Wegner, 1991), although effects of aging on posterior callosal regions have also been reported (Cowell, Allen, Zalatimo, & Denenberg, 1992). Evidence for gender differences in the effects of aging on the corpus callosum is inconsistent. Some studies have found greater effects for men than for women (Burke & Yeo, 1994; Johnson, Farnworth, Pinkston, Bigler, & Blatter, 1994; Witelson, 1989, 1991), whereas other studies have shown the opposite pattern (Salat et al., 1997) or no differences between men and women (Hayakawa et al., 1989; Parashos et al., 1995; Pozzilli et al., 1994; Witelson, 1989). Such variations among studies can be attributed to relatively small sample sizes in some cases, to variations in measurement techniques, and to the age ranges being examined. Cowell et al. (1992) described complex changes in callosal morphometry over the life span that can only be accurately understood when callosal subregion, gender, and age are taken into account. Indeed, in a meta-analysis performed on 21 studies of aging effects on the corpus callosum and including a sample of participants varying between 25 and 78 years of age, the average correlation (based on a less conservative estimate technique) was only $r = -0.16$ (Driesen & Raz, 1995). Therefore, we are left to conclude that any age-related declines in callosal size that exist are relatively small and may be restricted to the most anterior regions of the corpus callosum.

FUNCTIONS OF THE CORPUS CALLOSUM

The corpus callosum mediates interactions between the hemispheres that are essential for many aspects of human behavior (Gazzaniga, Bogen, & Sperry, 1962). Sensory information arriving in one hemisphere is transferred to the other hemisphere by way of the corpus callosum. Likewise, motor programs originating in the left or right hemispheres can be transferred to the opposite side via the callosum. When the corpus callosum is damaged—for example, through a cerebrovascular event or when it is severed for treatment of epilepsy (i.e., callosotomy)—distinct disconnection deficits are evident. These deficits typically include the inability to match visual stimuli presented to the left visual field (LVF) and right visual field (RVF) or to the left and right hands and, in left-hemisphere-dominant individuals, the inability to name items presented to the left hand or LVF and the loss of the ability to write (agraphia) with the left hand (Bogen, 1993; Geschwind & Kaplan, 1962; Reuter-Lorenz & Miller, 1998; Seymour, Reuter-Lorenz, & Gazzaniga, 1994).

In addition to transferring sensory information and motor commands between the two hemispheres, the corpus callosum also plays an important role in higher cognitive processes. Studies of patients who have undergone callosotomy have suggested that the corpus callosum contributes to the efficient deployment of selective attention, the coordination of high-level plans, and the effective use of mnemonic strategies (for reviews, see Reuter-Lorenz, in press; Reuter-Lorenz & Miller, 1998). The precise mechanisms underlying these particular contributions of the corpus callosum to cognition are as yet unspecified. One possibility is that the corpus callosum is essential to modulatory processes that permit focal neural activity and the selective engagement of specific brain regions to perform specific cognitive operations (Kinsbourne, 1974). Evidence from neurologically intact individuals is mounting to suggest that the corpus callosum plays a critical role in the allocation of attentional resources and in *recruitment,* a process by which additional brain regions are engaged in information-processing operations to meet task demands (Banich, 1998; Liederman, 1998). In the following sections we review evidence that age affects sensorimotor transfer, and we consider the relation between aging and the attentional resource modulation functions of the callosum.

AGING AND SENSORIMOTOR TRANSFER

The time required to transfer sensorimotor signals from one hemisphere to the other has been estimated using a simple behavioral task, known in some circles as the Poffenberger (1912) paradigm (for a review, see Zaidel & Iacoboni, in press). This task requires a manual response (i.e., a key press) to the detection of a light flash presented to either the LVF or RVF. A key press made by the right index finger in response to a RVF flash is presumed not to require callosal transmission because the left hemisphere both receives the sensory input and generates the required motor output. The same is true for responses made by the left hand in response to a LVF flash of light. These are defined as the *uncrossed* conditions. In contrast, when the right index finger must press a key in response to a LVF flash, or when the left index finger must respond to a RVF flash, interhemispheric transfer is required. These conditions are defined as the *crossed* conditions. The requirement of interhemispheric transfer presumably takes additional processing time, resulting in longer reaction times (RTs) in the crossed than in the uncrossed conditions. Transfer time is estimated by subtracting the average RT for the uncrossed conditions from that obtained from the crossed conditions. This difference has come to be known as the crossed–uncrossed difference (CUD; for a review, see Marzi, Bisiacchi, & Niccoletti, 1991).

CUD estimates of interhemispheric transfer time in normal healthy young adults are on the order of 3 msec to 4 msec (e.g., Marzi et al., 1991). The role of the corpus callosum in mediating the transfer associated with crossed RTs is supported by a number of studies that have examined the effects of partial or complete callosal section on the magnitude of the CUD (for reviews, see Reuter-Lorenz, Nozawa, Gazzaniga, & Hughes, 1995; Saron & Davidson, 1989). Patients with complete callosal section or with partial section restricted to the anterior two thirds show a substantial increase in the CUD, ranging from 30 msec to 60 msec or more depending on the individual patient (e.g., Aglioti, Berlucchi, Pallini, Rossi, & Tassinari, 1993; Clark & Zaidel, 1989).

It should be noted that the relation between CUD estimates of transfer and the underlying neural events is far from straightforward. One indication of the complexity of this relation comes from the work of Saron, Vaughan, Foxe, and Simpson (in press), who used high-density electrode placements on the human scalp to measure the timing of electrophysiological events (i.e., event-related potentials [ERPs]) in the Poffenberger (1912) paradigm. They reported evidence of numerous interhemispheric volleys between visual and association cortices, as well as between motor areas that contribute differentially to the response time evident at the effector.

Nonetheless, there are indications that the CUD may be affected by aging. Recent work by Jeeves and Moes (1996) showed that healthy adults between the ages of 60 and 82 years show a significant increase in the magnitude of the CUD compared to younger adults. Hoptman, Davidson, Gudmundsson, Schreiber, and Ershler (1996) were unsuccessful in demonstrating this RT pattern in a different sample of older adults (in the same age range as that studied by Jeeves & Moes, 1996) and somewhat surprisingly found that older adults responded as rapidly overall as the younger group. Their ERP measures of sensorimotor events were more revealing, however. Typically, the early components of the ERPs, such as the P100, are smaller in the hemisphere ipsilateral to the stimulated visual field (crossed condition) compared to those recorded from the contralateral hemisphere (uncrossed condition; for a review, see Hoptman et al., 1996). This difference is attributed to the reduction in signal strength that accompanies the callosal relay of sensory information to the ipsilateral hemisphere. Hoptman et al. found that the amplitudes of the contralateral waveforms did not differ in older and younger adults, but that the amplitudes of the ipsilateral waveforms were significantly smaller in the older group than in the younger group. Although the latencies of the waveforms were similar in the two age groups, the amplitude difference suggests that aging adversely affects the quality of interhemispheric interactions. Moreover, the neural generators of the P100 peak that showed the age difference are thought to reside in the visual cortex, suggesting that aging compromises the quality of callosally mediated sensory interactions. It is unclear why this electrophysiological difference did not manifest itself behaviorally.

Aging may influence interhemispheric control of motor performance as well. Moes, Jeeves, and Cook (1995) tested this possibility using drawing tests of bimanual coordination. The tests were based on Preilowski's (1972) studies of the effects of commissurotomy on the performance of bimanual tasks. Preilowski showed that hemispheric separation has the most adverse effects on tasks that require asymmetrical motor output when performance is unaided by visual feedback. One example of such a task would be drawing a line at a 30° angle using a device like an Etch-a-Sketch™. Moes et al. found the greatest age deficits on these types of tasks, suggesting that aging adversely affects the interhemispheric interactions that mediate bimanual coordination (see also Stelmach, Amrhein, & Goggin, 1988; cf. Weller & Latimer-Sayer, 1985).

THE CALLOSUM AND ATTENTIONAL ALLOCATION

In addition to mediating the transmission of sensorimotor signals, evidence from divided visual field studies with young adults suggests that the corpus callosum may contribute to the allocation of resources that are needed to meet the cognitive demands of complex tasks. A variety of reports suggest that lateralized processing by one or the other hemisphere can suffice for easy tasks, but that difficult tasks are performed more efficiently when both hemispheres contribute (Liederman, 1986; Norman, Jeeves, Milner, & Ludwig, 1992; for a review, see Liederman, 1998).

This effect is beautifully illustrated in a series of experiments by Banich and her colleagues (Banich & Belger, 1990; Belger & Banich, 1992). In one study, for example, observers performed a series of letter-matching tasks that varied in complexity (Figure 1). In the simplest task, the observer judged whether the uppercase

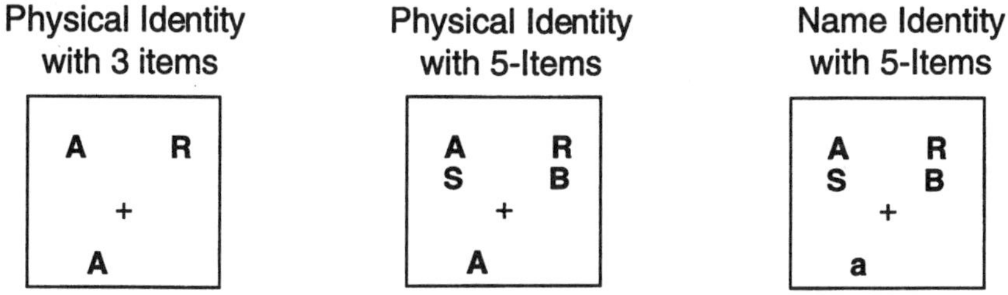

FIGURE 1 Sample displays illustrating within-hemisphere match trials for each of three levels of task complexity. The target letter always appeared at the bottom of the display, and the probe letters were in the upper rows of the displays. In the physical-identity match trials, the target letter physically matched one of the probes (in this example, A-A). In the name-identity match trials, the target letter had the same name as one of the probes (in this example, a-A).

target letter in the lower row of the display was physically identical to either of the two uppercase probes in the upper row. The next level of complexity required detection of a physical match between the target letter and one of four probe letters, two in each visual field. The most complex task again had four probes and required a match based on letter name. Thus, the target appeared in lowercase and the probes were uppercase.

Although probe letters always appeared in both visual fields, the critical manipulation involved the relative location of the target letter and the matching probe letter (see Figure 2). When the target and matching probe appeared in opposite visual fields (across-hemisphere match), both hemispheres contributed to the determination of a match. In this sense, the across-hemisphere match condition recruits bihemispheric processing and requires interhemispheric communication to determine the presence of a match. In the within-hemisphere condition, the match could be performed by a single hemisphere because the matching letters appeared in the same visual field. Interhemispheric interactions are not essential in this condition. For the simplest task, observers were faster and more accurate in the within-hemisphere condition than the across-hemisphere condition. However, as task complexity increased, this pattern reversed, such that performance in the across-hemisphere condition was superior to that of the within-hemisphere condition.

Belger and Banich (1992) explained this interaction between trial type (within- or across-hemisphere) and task complexity by considering the cost associated with interhemispheric transmission relative to the benefit of additional resources made available when the target and matching probe are processed by different hemispheres. For easier tasks, the neural resources available unilaterally are sufficient. As a result, the benefits of within-hemisphere processing exceed the cost of interhemispheric transfer required for across-hemisphere matches. However, more difficult tasks impose greater cognitive demands, which are met more ef-

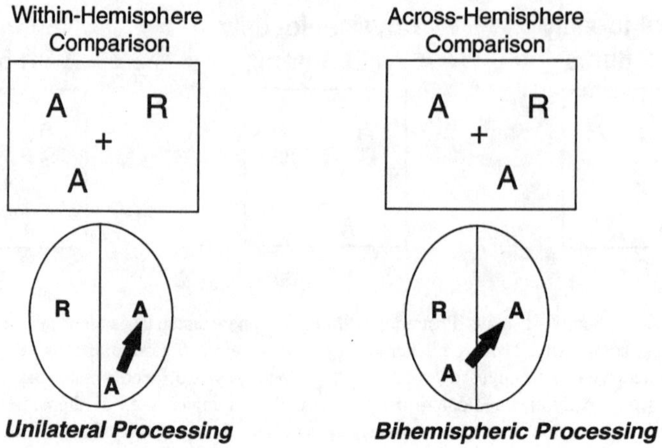

FIGURE 2 A schematic illustrating the within-hemisphere and across-hemisphere trial types. For within-hemisphere trial types, the target and probe were presented in the same visual field and projected to the same hemisphere, in which case a match could be detected without the need for interhemispheric interactions. For the across-hemisphere trial types, the target and probe were presented to opposite visual fields and projected to different hemispheres, in which case match detection required that the two hemispheres interact (based on Belger & Banich, 1992).

fectively by bilateral processing. In this case, the benefits from engaging the resources of both hemispheres to process the target and matching probe presumably exceed any costs associated with the added requirement of interhemispheric communication (see also, Banich, 1998). The across-hemisphere match condition recruits resources from both hemispheres to a greater extent than within-hemisphere matches do. Bilateral resources are advantageous for more difficult tasks, leading to a performance advantage on across-hemisphere trials. Banich (1998) argued for an attentional basis for the across-hemisphere advantage based on several corroborating findings, including the fact that this effect is found for auditory and tactile versions of the matching task and when the nature of the attentional demands is specifically varied, as in a feature versus conjunction search task.

AGING AND ATTENTIONAL FUNCTIONS OF THE CALLOSUM

How may age affect performance in this task? One possibility is that decreased efficiency of the corpus callosum would cause a general disadvantage in the across-hemisphere condition for older adults. An alternative possibility is that a general decrease in processing resources in the older brain leads to a greater dependence on resources made available from bihemispheric processing. In this case, the performance of older adults may actually improve in across-hemisphere conditions.

We recently tested these predictions and found evidence in favor of the latter hypothesis (Reuter-Lorenz, Stanczak, & Miller, 1999). A group of 19 older adults (aged 65–75 years) and a group of 23 younger adults (aged 18–25 years) performed the three types of letter-matching tasks described previously. Across all three levels of computational complexity, older adults were slower and less accurate than the younger group. To evaluate the effects of age on interhemispheric interactions, we compared performance of each age group on within-hemisphere and across-hemisphere matches. Contrary to the idea that there is a general decline in callosal function with age, we found that the older adults were generally better in the across-hemisphere conditions than in the within-hemisphere conditions. Their across-hemisphere advantage was evident in the RT and accuracy data for the intermediate and highest complexity conditions. In the low-complexity condition, both older and younger groups showed statistically equivalent and reliable within-hemisphere advantages for RT. The younger group showed a reliable RT advantage in the across-hemisphere condition only for the highest level of task complexity.

Several aspects of these results deserve comment. First, the data provide no indication that older adults are disadvantaged by the requirement for interhemispheric interaction imposed by the across-hemisphere matching condition. On the contrary, performance of older adults was generally optimized by bihemispheric processing. Second, the older group showed a greater across-hemisphere advantage than did the younger group in the intermediate-complexity condition, suggesting that older adults benefit from bihemispheric processing at lower levels of task complexity than their younger counterparts. The tendency for older adults to display a greater bihemispheric processing advantage than younger adults persisted in the high-complexity condition, where an across-hemisphere advantage was evident for both groups but was greater for older adults. In sum, these data provide no indication that older adults are specifically disadvantaged by the requirement for interhemispheric interaction.

Our results, therefore, challenge the idea that there is a general decline in callosal functioning as we age. Indeed, the results suggest an interesting alternative possibility: Aging has differential effects on callosal functions. Whereas certain sensorimotor functions of the callosum may decline disproportionately with age, aging may involve an increased reliance on the attentional and resource allocation functions of this structure. Thus, the effects of aging on callosal functions may be dissociable. In support of this possibility, we here report evidence from a subgroup of older and younger adults who participated in the experiment by Reuter-Lorenz et al. (1999) and who also participated in a replication of the simple RT experiment reported by Jeeves and Moes (1996). Like Jeeves and Moes, we find a greater CUD in older adults than in younger adults. It is important to note that in across-hemisphere letter-matching conditions that required interhemispheric interactions, this same group of older adults showed benefits that were equal to or exceeded those observed in the younger group.

METHOD

Participants

Twenty-three healthy older adults (aged 65–75 years, 11 men, 12 women) and 20 younger adults (aged 18–25 years, 10 men, 10 women) participated in this study. Older adults were recruited through the University of Michigan Institute of Gerontology and were paid for their time. Younger adults were recruited through the University's participant pools and either received course credit or were paid for their time. All participants had a minimum of 12 years of education and were categorized as consistent right-handers based on their responses to the Edinburgh Handedness Inventory (Oldfield, 1971). All participants were free of positive neurological histories and had normal or corrected to normal vision.

Apparatus

A Macintosh PowerPC with PsyScope software (Cohen, MacWhinney, Flatt, & Provost, 1993) was used for stimulus presentation and data acquisition. Each participant sat comfortably with his or her chin in a headrest to ensure a constant viewing distance of 57 cm.

Simple Reaction Time Task Design and Procedure

A red uppercase *X* was centered on a black background of the computer screen and remained visible throughout each experimental block. A white circle (approximately 0.5° × 0.5°) served as the command stimulus to which the participants responded. It appeared 5.25° to the left or right of the fixation point. Testing was conducted in a dark room with the lights out. Participants responded by pressing the space bar with the index finger of the designated response hand. They were instructed to keep their entire forearm resting comfortably on the desk in front of them to maximize the use of the distal musculature in generating the key-press response.

Participants were instructed to maintain their gaze on the central fixation stimulus throughout each trial. A trial began with the simultaneous onset of a 200-msec warning tone and the blink of the fixation point. After an interval that varied randomly between 500 msec and 1,000 msec (in 100-msec increments), the command stimulus appeared for 50 msec. The stimulus was equally likely to appear in the LVF or RVF. Approximately 14% of the trials were catch trials in which no target occurred and participants were to refrain from responding. There was an interval of 1 sec between trials. The testing session began with a practice block of 42 trials for each hand. This was followed by four 70-trial experimental runs, two for each hand. Participants then completed the letter-matching task (see following) in its entirety before performing four more blocks (two for each hand) to complete the simple RT task. Blocks for each response hand were run in a counterbalanced order between participants.

Response times faster than 200 msec and longer than 700 msec were designated as outliers, amounting to less than 1% of the data for each group. Four means for each participant were calculated based on the remaining data set: left-hand–LVF target, left-hand–RVF target, right-hand–LVF target, right-hand–RVF target.

Letter-Matching Task Design

Three experimental tasks varied in complexity: three-item physical identity (3-PI), five-item physical identity (5-PI), and five-item name identity (5-NI). In the 3-PI task, all letters were uppercase, and the target letter could physically match one of the two probe letters. In the 5-PI task, all letters were uppercase, and the target letter could physically match one of the four probe letters. In the 5-NI task, the target letter was lowercase and the probes were uppercase, so matches were based on nominal identity.

In each stimulus display, the target letter appeared 1.4° below and 1.4° to the left or right of a central fixation cross. In the 3-PI task, the two probe letters appeared 1.4° above the fixation point and 2.8° left or right of the fixation point (one letter in each visual field; see Figure 1). In the 5-PI and 5-NI tasks, the four probe letters were positioned in two rows, 1.9° and 0.87° above the fixation point, with each letter appearing 2.8° lateral to the midline (two letters in each visual field). Each letter (Geneva font) subtended a maximum of 0.85° horizontally and 1.2° vertically. Targets and probes were randomly chosen from the following set: A, B, D, F, G, H, M, N, R, S, T.

The target appeared randomly with equal probability in the LVF or RVF. On one half of the trials, the target matched one of the probe letters, and on the other half of the trials, there was no match. On match trials, the matching probe was equally likely to appear in the same visual field and hemisphere as the target (within-hemisphere match trials) or in the visual field and hemisphere opposite to the target (across-hemisphere match trials).

Procedure

Participants were instructed to maintain fixation on the central cross throughout each trial. A blink of the fixation cross and a short beep marked the start of each trial. After 500 msec, the letter array appeared for 200 msec. A go–no-go procedure was used. Participants were instructed to respond quickly (without compromising accuracy) only if the target letter matched one of the probe letters above the fixation point. They responded by pressing the space bar with their right index fingers during the 2-sec response interval. The three tasks were blocked, and their order was counterbalanced between participants. One practice and three experimental blocks, each consisting of 64 trials, were performed for each task.

RESULTS

Simple Reaction Time Task

The RT data were analyzed using a three-way analysis of variance (ANOVA), with *age group* (younger, older) as a between-subject factor and with *hand* (left, right) and *visual field* (LVF, RVF) as within-subjects factors.[1] Older participants were significantly slower than the younger group, $F(1, 41) = 16.603, p < .0002$ ($M = 329, SE = 5.2$; $M = 282, SE = 2.2$, respectively). There was also a significant interaction between age group and visual field, $F(1, 41) = 4.006, p < .052$. This effect was due to the fact that the younger group showed no difference between LVF and RVF RTs (average 281 and 283, respectively), whereas the older group showed faster responses to RVF than to LVF targets (average 326 and 332, respectively). The interaction between response hand and visual field was significant, $F(1, 41) = 9.607, p < .0035$, reflecting the expected left-hand advantage for LVF targets and right-hand advantage for RVF targets. Most important, however, is the significant three-way interaction indicating that the interaction of hand and visual field was reliably different in the two age groups, $F(1, 41) = 4.079, p = .050$. The means and standard errors for each hand–visual field combination for older and younger adults are listed in Table 1. Older adults showed an RT advantage for the uncrossed (ipsilateral) hand–visual field combinations compared with the crossed (contralateral) conditions. This uncrossed advantage was due primarily to the data for the right hand, where there was a 13-msec difference between the RVF and LVF conditions, $t(22) = 4.68, p < .001$.[2] The CUD for the left hand was a minimal 1.7 msec, which is far from statistical significance. Younger adults showed no reliable differences between the crossed and uncrossed conditions for either the left or the right hand (both had p values greater than .10). Nevertheless, the small magnitude of the CUD for young adults is in line

---

[1]Across both age groups, women tended to respond more slowly than men ($p = .054$). However, the variable of gender did not interact with age or any other variable and is not considered further.

[2]Expressing the crossed–uncrossed difference (CUD) as a proportion of each participant's mean reaction time resulted in a significant difference between older and younger adults overall (mean proportional CUD for older adults = .023 and for younger adults = .0056; $t[41] = 1.99, p < .03$, for the right hand alone (older = .038 and younger = –.0009; $t[41] = 3.92, p < .001$), but not for the left hand alone.

TABLE 1
Average Response Times and Standard Error Scores (in Milliseconds) for Younger and Older Participants in Each Task for Each Hand by Visual Field Combination and the Crossed–Uncrossed Difference for Each Hand

	Left Hand						*Right Hand*					
	LVF		*RVF*		*CUD*		*LVF*		*RVF*		*CUD*	
Group	*M*	*SE*	*M*	*SE*	*M*	*SE*	*M*	*SE*	*M*	*SE*	*M*	*SE*
Younger	281.37	4.75	284.65	3.78	3.28	—	281.02	4.74	281.20	4.48	–0.18	—
Older	327.49	10.5	329.22	9.65	1.73	—	336.69	11.55	323.72	10.29	12.97	—

Note. LVF = left visual field; RVF = right visual field; CUD = crossed–uncrossed difference.

with the data reported by Jeeves and Moes (1996). They found a 4-msec CUD for the right hand and a 1-msec CUD for the left hand. Likewise, the 13-msec right-hand CUD we found in older adults is in line with the 12-msec effect Jeeves and Moes found for the right hand in their older group. Their group of older adults, like ours, had a small, nonsignificant CUD for the left hand (approximately 3 msec).

The error rates (misses and false alarms) on this task were very low for both groups, averaging 1.2% errors for older participants and 0.81% errors for younger participants. This difference was not reliable ($p > .30$).

Letter-Matching Task

As described in Reuter-Lorenz et al. (1999), individuals were required to have a minimum d' of 1.0 on all three letter-matching tasks to be included in our analyses. Of the 43 adults who participated in the simple RT task, 41 also participated in the letter-matching task. Eighteen younger and 17 older adults from this group met the letter-matching performance criterion. The accuracy data for match trials were classified as within-hemisphere or across-hemisphere and were submitted to an ANOVA with *task complexity* (3-PI, 5-PI, 5-NI), *trial type* (within-hemisphere, across-hemisphere), and *age group* as factors.[3] For the accuracy data, errors tended to increase as task complexity increased, $F(2, 33) = 43.85, p = .0001$. Overall, older adults made more errors than the younger group, $F(1, 33) = 35.39, p < .0001$, with the age-related differences in accuracy being larger for the two more complex tasks compared to the simplest task, $F(2, 66) = 11.002, p < .0001$ (see Table 2). Of greatest relevance here is the significant interaction between age group and trial type, $F(1, 33) = 7.06, p < .012$. Younger adults showed no accuracy difference due to trial type. In contrast, older adults were more accurate overall in the across-hemisphere

[3]The results for this subgroup of participants were similar in all respects to the results from the larger data set reported in Reuter-Lorenz, Stanczak, and Miller (1999).

TABLE 2
Average Percentage Correct and Standard Error Scores for Younger and Older Participants in Each Task Under Within-Hemisphere and Across-Hemisphere Conditions and the Average of These Conditions

	3-PI		*5-PI*		*5-NI*	
Group	*M*	*SE*	*M*	*SE*	*M*	*SE*
Younger						
Within-hemisphere	98.12	0.54	94.67	0.80	88.69	1.65
Across-hemisphere	97.99	0.62	94.02	0.98	90.18	1.36
Combined	98.05	0.41	94.35	0.63	89.43	1.07
Older						
Within-hemisphere	92.38	2.05	73.06	3.37	69.25	2.18
Across-hemisphere	95.18	0.75	79.06	2.75	76.53	2.41
Combined	93.78	1.10	76.07	2.19	72.89	1.67

Note. 3-PI = three-item physical identity; 5-PI = five-item physical identity; 5-NI = five-item name identity.

condition. The high levels of accuracy for the younger group, particularly in the simplest task, reduces the sensitivity of this measure for that group. However, for the older group there was a strong accuracy advantage in the across-hemisphere condition, which would not be expected if there were a general age-related impairment in callosally mediated interhemispheric interactions. The three-way interaction of age, trial type, and task was not significant.

For the latency data, correct response times falling 2.5 *SD*s from the mean were treated as outliers and were eliminated from the data set (approximately 2% of all responses). A three-way ANOVA was performed with task, trial type, and age group as factors. Like the accuracy data, the RT data also challenge the generality of age-related callosal decline (see Table 3). Once again, task complexity influenced performance such that response times increased with increasing task complexity, $F(2, 33) = 76.96$, $p < .0001$, and older participants were slower overall than the younger group, $F(1, 33) = 9.898$, $p < .0005$. The RT difference between older and younger participants was smaller for the simple task than for the two more complex tasks, as indicated by the significant interaction of age group and task complexity, $F(2, 33) = 3.13$, $p < .05$. Most relevant for this report, however, was the significant interaction between task complexity and trial type, $F(2, 66) = 10.46$, $p < .0001$. As Banich and her colleagues (see Banich, 1998, for a review) have shown, for the simplest task, response times are faster for the within-hemisphere condition than for the across-hemisphere condition. This pattern reverses as task complexity increases. For both the intermediate and highest levels of complexity, the across-hemisphere condition produced faster response times than the within-hemisphere condition. This change from a within-hemisphere to an across-hemisphere advantage with increasing complexity was evident for both age groups and suggests that the advantage

TABLE 3
Average Response Times and Standard Error Scores (in Milliseconds) for Younger and Older Participants in Each Task Under Within-Hemisphere and Across-Hemisphere Conditions and the Average of These Conditions

	3-PI		*5-PI*		*5-NI*	
Group	*M*	*SE*	*M*	*SE*	*M*	*SE*
Younger						
Within-hemisphere	487	15.30	551	12.27	672	21.56
Across-hemisphere	501	14.87	539	9.98	647	21.33
Combined	494	10.63	545	7.90	660	15.13
Older						
Within-hemisphere	572	17.25	721	26.66	798	23.87
Across-hemisphere	593	18.06	693	27.05	771	26.07
Combined	583	12.46	707	18.93	784	17.62

Note. 3-PI = three-item physical identity; 5-PI = five-item physical identity; 5-NI = five-item name identity.

accrued from bihemispheric processing outweighs the costs of callosally mediated interactions in the across-hemisphere condition. If age-related decline affected all callosal functions, older adults should have benefited less, if at all, from bihemispheric processing, compared to the younger group.

Reuter-Lorenz et al. (1999) reported that the across-hemisphere advantage emerges at a lower level of task complexity for the older group than the younger group in that for both accuracy and RT older participants show a reliable across-hemisphere advantage for the intermediate and complex tasks, whereas the younger group shows this effect only for the most complex task. Although it is not the focus of this report, the same pattern of results is evident in this study's subset of data (see Tables 2 and 3), particularly for accuracy, where the older group is better in the across- than the within-hemisphere condition for all tasks, whereas younger adults show only a hint of this pattern for the most complex task. For the RT data in the intermediate task, the across-hemisphere advantage for the older group is more than twice that observed in the younger group, suggesting that the across-hemisphere advantage emerges at lower levels of task complexity as we age. On the basis of this pattern, we suggest that for all but the simplest tasks, performance can be optimized in older adults by recruiting the additional resources made available in the across-hemisphere condition.

Correlations Between Letter-Matching and Simple RT Performance

To determine whether there was any relation between the advantage from bihemispheric processing in the letter-matching task and the CUD measure of simple RT performance, a series of correlations were performed on the data from the older and younger groups. We focused on the CUD scores for the right hand because this score showed an age-related effect of interhemispheric interaction, whereas the left-hand score did not. Moreover, the right hand was used for responding in the letter-matching task, so analyzing the same response hand for the simple RT task should offer the most sensitive test of whether or not these measures are related. For the letter-matching task, we calculated the difference between the within-hemisphere latency and across-hemisphere latency for each task separately. Within- minus across-hemisphere difference scores were also derived for the accuracy data for each letter-matching task.

How may these different measures of interhemispheric interaction be related in the older participants? If aging brings about a general and unitary decline in callosal functioning, then we may expect that a larger CUD would be associated with poorer performance on across- than on within-hemisphere matching (reflected in a weaker across-hemisphere advantage, particularly for more complex tasks). Alternatively, a greater CUD may be indicative of declining neural efficiency more generally. Likewise, a tendency to benefit from across-hemisphere conditions in the matching task may arise from the need to recruit resources from both hemispheres, a need that could stem from widespread decreases in neural efficiency. According to this scenario, the magnitude of the CUD and the magnitude of the across-hemisphere advantage would be positively related, particularly for more complex tasks. Finally, there may be no relation between these measures because they reflect different and dissociable aspects of callosal function.

For simplicity, all of the difference scores for the letter-matching task were calculated as the within-hemisphere minus the across-hemisphere condition. One must bear in mind, however, that the CUD score is the crossed minus the uncrossed condition. No significant relation emerged for older adults between the CUD measure of callosal function and the across-within difference scores in the letter-matching task (see Table 4). Only two of these correlations were greater than .20, and these were far from significance. The right CUD score was positively correlated with the RT difference score for the 5-NI task, $r(17) = .290, p = .20$. This means that as the CUD increased, the across-hemisphere RT advantage also increased, although not significantly. Similarly, the CUD score was negatively correlated with the accuracy difference score for the 5-NI letter-matching task, indicating that as the CUD increased, the across-hemisphere accuracy advantage also increased. Again, this relation was not significant, $r(18) = -.325; p = .26$. We note that for younger adults neither of these correlations were greater than .10, and none of the correlations with the right CUD were greater than .20 (see Table 5).

As with any null result, of course, the absence of reliable effects must be interpreted with caution, particularly given our relatively small sample size. The need for caution is underscored by the observation that even the correlations between seemingly related measures (e.g., within RT – across RT for 5-PI and 5-NI tasks)

TABLE 4

Correlations of Difference Scores for Older Adults Who Participated in Both the Simple Reaction Time and Letter-Matching Tasks and Met the Performance Criteria for the Latter

Difference Measure	*RCUD*	*W – A.3-PI.RT*	*W – A.5-PI.RT*	*W – A.5-NI.RT*	*W – A.3-PI.%*	*W – A.5-PI.%*	*W – A.5-NI.%*
RCUD	1.000						
W – A.3-PI.RT	–0.075	1.000					
W – A.5-PI.RT	–0.127	0.369	1.000				
W – A.5-NI.RT	0.290	0.419	0.258	1.000			
W – A.3-PI.%	–0.155	–0.493	–0.193	–0.244	1.000		
W – A.5-PI.%	0.034	–0.351	–0.344	–0.063	0.431	1.000	
W – A.5-NI.%	–0.325	0.104	0.057	–0.247	0.416	0.183	1.000

Note. RCUD is the average crossed minus uncrossed reaction time (RT) for the right hand. The remaining difference measures are the averaged within (W) minus the averaged across (A) hemisphere RT and accuracy (%) for the three-item physical identity (3-PI), five-item physical identity (5-PI), and five-item name identity (5-PI) tasks. $N = 17$.

TABLE 5

Correlations of Difference Scores for Younger Adults Who Participated in Both the Simple Reaction Time and Letter-Matching Tasks and Met the Performance Criteria for the Latter

Difference Measure	*RCUD*	*W – A.3-PI.RT*	*W – A.5-PI.RT*	*W – A.5-NI.RT*	*W – A.3-PI.%*	*W – A.5-PI.%*	*W – A.5-NI.%*
RCUD	1.000						
W – A.3-PI.RT	0.147	1.000					
W – A.5-PI.RT	0.180	0.062	1.000				
W – A.5-NI.RT	0.039	0.328	–0.193	1.000			
W – A.3-PI.%	0.112	–0.622	0.090	–0.369	1.000		
W – A.5-PI.%	–0.048	–0.181	–0.340	–0.075	0.124	1.000	
W – A.5-NI.%	0.035	–0.115	0.151	–0.271	0.008	–0.064	1.000

Note. RCUD is the average crossed minus uncrossed reaction time (RT) for the right hand. The remaining difference measures are the averaged within (W) minus the averaged across (A) hemisphere RT and accuracy (%) for the three-item physical identity (3-PI), five-item physical identity (5-PI), and five-item name identity (5-PI) tasks. $N = 18$.

are only weakly related (r = .258). Nevertheless, there is little evidence that a larger CUD is associated with poorer across-hemisphere matching performance. If anything, the data suggest the opposite pattern: The greater the CUD, the greater the across-hemisphere advantage in letter-matching performance.

DISCUSSION

Our results show for the first time that different functions of the corpus callosum are differentially affected by the aging process. Performance on a speeded motor task thought to rely on the interhemispheric transmission of visuomotor signals is adversely affected by aging. In contrast, on a letter-matching task requiring the processing of letter identity information, callosal contributions appear to be relatively preserved. It is important to bear in mind that on the simple motor task and on the matching tasks, older adults performed more poorly overall than younger adults. Our focus, however, for both tasks, is on comparing performance under conditions that require interhemispheric interactions with performance in conditions that do not. The important result is that the requirement for interhemispheric interactions disadvantages older adults in the sensorimotor task but not in the letter-matching task. Indeed, in the letter-matching task, the interhemispheric interaction requirement benefits performance in older adults more so than in the younger adults.

Our results from the sensorimotor task replicate the effect reported by Jeeves and Moes (1996). Although Hoptman et al. (1996) reported age differences in the amplitude of the visual evoked responses on crossed trials in a similar task, they found no behavioral differences between their older and younger participants. Their electrophysiological results suggest that callosally mediated transfer of visual signals may be adversely affected by aging, however, this result is somewhat ambiguous in the absence of a behavioral difference between the groups. Moreover, it is important to bear in mind that there are numerous interhemispheric volleys associated with even this relatively simple task (Saron et al., in press). Visual transfer via the splenium and motoric interactions via the midbody of the corpus callosum are likely to mediate this task. Aging could affect several or all of these callosally mediated processes. Thus, finding a greater CUD in older than in younger adults does not tell us precisely which part of the callosum is affected, but it does indicate a domain of functions that may be particularly vulnerable to aging.

Likewise, the interhemispheric processes evoked in Banich's (e.g., Belger & Banich, 1992) letter-matching tasks are also difficult to localize at present. Based on converging evidence from a variety of divided visual field studies in neurologically intact young adults, Banich (1998) has argued that this task reveals the importance of interhemispheric interactions for modulating the brain's attentional capacity or processing resources. Frontal and parietal sites involved in the cortical attention system are likely candidates for callosal channels that are relevant to these tasks. These channels would course through the genu and through the isthmus-splenial regions, respectively. To the extent that aging is associated with widespread decreases in processing efficiency, it may be accompanied by a greater need to recruit additional resources for any given task in older adults than in younger adults. The present results suggest that this aspect of callosal function is relatively preserved in older adults who show functional decline in sensorimotor transfer.

Structure–Function Relations

The present results indicate that aging has different effects on different functions of the corpus callosum. How do these results fit with the evidence for structural decline of the anterior corpus callosum? Because both tasks are likely to rely to some extent on anterior callosal pathways, the fact that one task shows functional decline and the other does not presents a bit of a conundrum. Several issues are relevant to evaluating this puzzle. First, as reviewed in the introduction to this article, the evidence for age-related callosal atrophy is somewhat weak, suggesting that these effects are either small, highly variable, or both. Second, even if both tasks rely on the anterior callosum, it is likely that they rely on different pathways within this callosal subregion. It is conceivable that some callosal pathways are more affected by aging than others are, even within a particular callosal subregion. The present results recommend the use of a combined behavioral–anatomic approach. We may expect, for example, that the individuals with the greatest CUD would show the greatest signs of callosal decline in particular subregions. Likewise, individuals showing the greatest advantage of bihemispheric processing may show the greatest preservation in other callosal subregions. Clearly, further research is needed to establish the precise pathways and mechanisms associated with these interhemispheric processes and the extent to which alterations in these processes affect cognitive aging.

Callosal Changes and Functional Imaging

Recent neuroimaging work provides further indications that interhemispheric interactions are critical to aging effects. For example, Reuter-Lorenz et al. (2000) found bilateral activation in older adults on tasks for which younger adults show lateralized activity, and these age differences are greatest in the frontal lobes. One task was a verbal working memory task that required the retention of four letters for 3 sec. For both age groups, this task evoked left-hemisphere activation in frontal and parietal sites that have been linked with the rehearsal and storage of verbal information. The older adults also showed significant activation in several anterior loci in the right hemisphere (Broca's area, dorsolateral prefrontal cortex), whereas younger adults did not. Likewise, in a spatial memory task requiring the short-term retention of several spatial locations, older adults showed left and right anterior activation, whereas in younger adults, frontal activity was right lateralized.

There are also other neuroimaging reports of age-related alterations in the pattern of lateralized activity during retrieval from long-term memory. Whereas young adults typically show right anterior activation under these conditions, older adults show left-hemisphere activation, which in some cases is accompanied by marked reductions in right-hemisphere activity relative to the younger group (Cabeza et al., 1997; Cabeza et al., 2000; Madden et al., 1999).

The functional implications of age-related changes in patterns of lateralized activation are presently unknown, although changes in callosally mediated interhemispheric interactions are likely to be involved in each of several alternative mechanisms. One possibility is that bilateral activation is dysfunctional and reflects a declining ability to selectively engage lateralized mechanisms that are specialized for particular cognitive functions. For example, it has been hypothesized that left-hemisphere verbal processors normally inhibit homologous sites in the right hemisphere, thereby maintaining dominance in the verbal domain (Kinsbourne, 1974). Bilateral involvement could arise if such inhibitory interactions were impaired (e.g., Kinsbourne, 1974; see also Kinsbourne & Byrd, 1985). The activation of nonspecialized regions could interfere with processing, thereby contributing to cognitive decrement in older adults. Alternatively, changes in laterality could have functional benefits and could reflect compensatory processes that enable the aging brain to meet cognitive task demands. For example, greater bilaterality could result from recruitment of additional brain areas to compensate for decrements in the efficiency of specialized regions (Cabeza et al., 1997; Grady, Haxby, Horwitz, Schapiro, & Rapoport, 1992; Madden et al., 1999; Reuter-Lorenz, 2000).

Although further work is needed to establish whether these mechanisms contribute to the changes in lateralized activity in older adults, this study's results lend some credence to both possibilities. The sensorimotor task provides evidence for age-related impairment in interhemispheric interactions within at least one performance domain. However, the cognitive demands of the letter-matching tasks have greater relevance to the neuroimaging tasks described previously. Here, hemispheric interactions are intact, and recruitment is evident in older adults. These results suggest that at least some aspects of callosal functioning may be preserved and may play a more prominent role in the cognitive functioning of the aging brain. Although the present results alone cannot resolve these issues, they point to the need for further research on the effects of normal aging on the functions of the corpus callosum. Future studies that obtain structural measures of the corpus callosum along with functional measures of interhemispheric processing in the same individuals will illuminate the role of the corpus callosum in aging and will advance our understanding of the role of this structure in human cognition.

ACKNOWLEDGMENTS

This research was supported by the Center for Applied Cognitive Research on Aging, one of the Edward R. Roybal Centers for Research in Applied Gerontology, funded through Grant AG11715–05 from the National Institute on Aging, and by Grant AG13027 from the National Institute on Aging.

We thank Andrea Miller and Joseph Mikels for their assistance with various aspects of this project, and Marie T. Banich and Warren S. Brown for their helpful critiques of an earlier version of this article. We are grateful for the comments and advice of Timothy Salthouse.

REFERENCES

Aboitiz, F., Scheibel, A., Fisher, R., & Zaidel, E. (1992a). Fiber composition of the human corpus callosum. *Brain Research, 598,* 143–153.

Aboitiz, F., Scheibel, A., Fisher, R., & Zaidel, E. (1992b). Individual difference in brain asymmetries and fiber composition in the human corpus callosum. *Brain Research, 598,* 154–161.

Aglioti, S., Berlucchi, G., Pallini, R., Rossi, G. F., & Tassinari, G. (1993). Hemispheric control of unilateral and bilateral responses to lateralized light stimuli after callosotomy and in callosal agenesis. *Experimental Brain Research, 93,* 151–165.

Allen, L. S., Richey, M. F., Chai, Y. M., & Gorski, R. A. (1991). Sex differences in the corpus callosum of the living human being. *Journal of Neuroscience, 11,* 933–942.

Banich, M. T. (1998). The missing link: The role of interhemispheric interaction in attentional processing. *Brain and Cognition, 36,* 128–157.

Banich, M. T., & Belger, A. (1990). Interhemispheric interactions: How do the hemispheres divide and conquer a task? *Cortex, 26,* 77–94.

Belger, A., & Banich, M. T. (1992). Interhemispheric interaction affected by computational complexity. *Neuropsychologia, 30,* 923–929.

Bogen, J. E. (1993). The callosal syndromes. In K. M. Heilman & E. Valenstein (Eds.), *Clinical neuropsychology* (3rd ed., pp. 337–407). New York: Oxford University Press.

Burke, H. L., & Yeo, R. A. (1994). Systematic variations in callosal morphology: The effects of age, gender, hand preference, and anatomic asymmetry. *Neuropsychology, 8,* 563–571.

Cabeza, R., Anderson, N. D., Houle, S., Mangels, J. A., & Nyberg, L. (2000). Age-related differences in neural activity during item and temporal-order memory retrieval: A positron emission tomography study. *Journal of Cognitive Neuroscience, 12,* 197–206.

Cabeza, R., Grady, C. L., Nyberg, L., McIntosh, A. R., Tulving, E., Kapur, S., Jennings, J. M., Houle, S., & Craik, F. I. (1997). Age-related differences in neural activity during memory encoding and retrieval: A positron emission tomography study. *Journal of Neuroscience, 17,* 391–400.

Clarke, J. M., & Zaidel, E. (1989). Simple reaction times to lateralized visual light flashes: Varieties of interhemispheric communication routes. *Brain, 112,* 849–870.

Cohen, J. D., MacWhinney, B., Flatt, M., & Provost, J. (1993). PsyScope: A new graphic interactive environment for designing psychology experiments. *Behavioral Research Methods, Instruments and Computers, 25,* 257–271.

Cowell, P. E., Allen, L. S., Zalatimo, N. S., & Denenberg, V. H. (1992). A developmental study of sex and age interactions in the human corpus callosum. *Developmental Brain Research, 66,* 187–192.

Craik, F. I. M., & Salthouse, T. A. (1992). *The handbook of aging and cognition.* Hillsdale, NJ: Lawrence Erlbaum Associates, Inc.

de Lacoste, M. C., Kirkpatrick, J. B., & Ross, E. D. (1985). Topography of the human corpus callosum. *Journal of Neuropathology and Experimental Neurology, 44,* 578–591.

Driesen, N. R., & Raz, N. (1995). The influence of sex, age, and handedness on corpus callosum morphology: A meta-analysis. *Psychobiology, 23,* 240–247.

Gazzaniga, M. S., Bogen J. E., & Sperry, R. W. (1962). Some functional effects of sectioning the cerebral commissures in man. *Proceedings of the National Academy of Sciences, USA, 48,* 1765–1769.

Geschwind, N., & Kaplan, E. (1962). A human cerebral deconnection syndrome. *Neurology, 12,* 675.

Grady, C. L., Haxby, J. V., Horwitz, B., Schapiro, M. B., & Rapoport, S. I. (1992). Dissociation of object and spatial vision in human extrastriate cortex: Age-related changes in activation of regional cerebral blood flow measured with [15 O] water and positron emission tomography. *Journal of Cognitive Neuroscience, 4,* 23–34.

Hartley, A. A. (1992). Attention. In F. I. M. Craik & T. A. Salthouse (Eds.), *The handbook of aging and cognition* (pp. 3–50). Hillsdale NJ: Lawrence Erlbaum Associates, Inc.

Hayakawa, K., Konishi, Y., Matsuda, T., Kuriyama, M., Konishi, K., Yamashita, K., Ogumura, R., & Hamanaka, D. (1989). Development and aging of brain midline structures: Assessment with MR imaging. *Radiology, 172,* 171–177.

Hopper, K. D., Patel, S., Cann, T. S., Wilcox, T., & Schaeffer, J. M. (1994). The relationship of age, gender, handedness, and sidedness to the size of the corpus callosum. *Academy of Radiology, 1,* 243–248.

Hoptman, M. J., Davidson, R. J., Gudmundsson, A., Schreiber, R. T., & Ershler, W. B. (1996). Age differences in visual evoked potential estimates on interhemispheric transfer. *Neuropsychology, 10,* 263–271.

Janowsky, J., Kaye, J. A., & Carper, R. A. (1996). Atrophy of the corpus callosum in Alzheimer's disease versus healthy aging. *Journal of the American Geriatric Society, 44,* 798–803.

Jeeves, M. A., & Moes, P. (1996). Interhemispheric transfer time differences related to aging and gender. *Neuropsychologia, 34,* 627–636.

Johnson, S. C., Farnworth, T., Pinkston, J. B., Bigler, E. D., & Blatter, D. D. (1994). Corpus callosum surface area across the human adult life span: Effect of age and gender. *Brain Research Bulletin, 35,* 373–377.

Kinsbourne, M. (1974). Mechanisms of hemispheric interaction in man. In M. Kinsbourne & W. L. Smith (Eds.), *Hemispheric disconnection and cerebral function* (pp. 260–285). Springfield, IL: Thomas.

Kinsbourne, M., & Byrd, M. (1984). Word load and visual hemifield shape recognition: Priming and interference effects. In M. I. Posner & O. Marin (Eds.), *Attention and performance* (pp. 529–543). Hillsdale, NJ: Lawrence Erlbaum Associates, Inc.

Liederman, J. (1986). Subtraction in addition to addition: Dual task performance improves when tasks are presented to separate hemispheres. *Journal of Clinical and Experimental Neuropsychology, 8,* 486–502.

Liederman, J. (1998). The dynamics of interhemispheric collaboration and hemispheric control. *Brain and Cognition, 36,* 193–208.

Madden, D. J., Turkington, T. G., Provenzale, J., Gottlob, L. R., Denny, L. L., Hawk, T. C., & Coleman, R. E. (1999). Adult age differences in the functional neuroanatomy of verbal recognition memory. *Human Brain Mapping, 7,* 115–135.

Marzi, C. A., Bisiacchi, P., & Niccoletti, R. (1991). Is interhemispheric transfer of visuomotor information asymmetric? Evidence from a meta-analysis. *Neuropsychologia, 29,* 1163–1177.

Moes, P., Jeeves, M. A., & Cook, K. (1995). Bimanual coordination with aging: Implications for interhemispheric transfer. *Developmental Neuropsychology, 11,* 23–40.

Norman, W. D., Jeeves, M. A., Milner, A., & Ludwig, T. (1992). Hemispheric interactions: The bilateral advantage and task difficulty. *Cortex, 28,* 623–642.

Oldfield, R. C. (1971). The assessment and analysis of handedness: The Edinburgh Inventory. *Neuropsychologia, 9,* 97–113.

Pandya, D. N., & Seltzer, B. (1986). The topography of commissural fibers. In F. Lepore, M. Ptito, & H. H. Jasper (Eds.), *Two hemispheres—one brain: Functions of the corpus callosum* (pp. 47–73). New York: Alan Liss.

Parashos, I. A., Wilkinson, W. E., & Coffey, C. E. (1995). Magnetic resonance imaging of the corpus callosum: Predictors of size in normal adults. *Journal of Neuropsychiatry, 7,* 35–41.

Park, D. C., Smith, A. D., Lautenschlager, G., Earles, J., Frieske, D., Zwahr, M., & Gaines, C. (1996). Mediators of long-term memory performance across the life span. *Psychology and Aging, 11,* 621–637.

Poffenberger, A. T. (1912). Reaction time to retinal stimulation with special reference to time lost in conducation through nerve centers. *Archives of Psychology, 23,* 1–73.

Pozzilli, C., Bastianello, S., Bozzao, A., Pierallini, A., Giubilei, F., Argentino, C., & Bozzao, L. (1994). No differences in callosal size by sex and aging: A quantitative study using magnetic resonance imaging. *Journal of Neuroimaging, 4,* 218–221.

Preilowski, B. F. B. (1972). Possible contribution of the anterior forebrain commissures to bilateral motor coordination. *Neuropsychologia, 10,* 267–277.

Reuter-Lorenz, P. A. (2000). Cognitive neuropsychology of aging. In D. Park & N. Schwarz (Eds.), *Primer of cognitive aging* (pp. 93–114). Philadelphia: Psychology Press.

Reuter-Lorenz, P. A. (in press). Attention and the bisected brain: Implications for an analysis of callosal function. In E. Zaidel & M. Iacoboni (Eds.), *The role of the corpus callosum in sensory-motor integration: Anatomy, physiology and behavior.* Cambridge, MA: MIT Press.

Reuter-Lorenz, P. A., Jonides, J., Smith, E., Hartley, A., Miller, A., Marshuetz, C., & Keoppe, R. (2000). Age differences in the frontal lateralization of verbal and spatial working memory revealed by PET. *Journal of Cognitive Neuroscience, 12,* 174–187.

Reuter-Lorenz, P. A., & Miller, A. (1998). The cognitive neuroscience of human laterality: Lessons from the bisected brain. *Current Directions in Psychological Science, 7,* 15–20.

Reuter-Lorenz, P. A., Nozawa, G., Gazzaniga, M. S., & Hughes, H. C. (1995). The fate of neglected targets in the callosotomized brain: A chronometric analysis. *Journal of Experimental Psychology: Human Perception and Performance, 21,* 211–230.

Reuter-Lorenz, P. A., Stanczak, L., & Miller, A. (1999). Neural recruitment and cognitive aging: Two hemispheres are better than one, especially as you age. *Psychological Science, 10,* 494–500.

Salat, D., Ward, A., Kaye, J. A., & Janowsky, J. S. (1997). Sex differences in the corpus callosum with aging. *Neurobiology of Aging, 18,* 1–7.

Salthouse, T. A. (1992). *Mechanisms of age–cognition relations in adulthood.* Hillsdale, NJ: Lawrence Erlbaum Associates, Inc.

Salthouse, T. A. (1996). General and specific speed mediation of adult age differences in memory. *Journals of Gerontology: Series B: Psychological Sciences and Social Sciences, 51B,* 30–42.

Saron, C. D., & Davidson, R. J. (1989). Reliability of evoked potential estimates of interhemispheric transfer time in humans. *Behavioral Neuroscience, 103,* 1115–1138.

Saron, C. D., Vaughan, H. G., Foxe, J. J., & Simpson, G. V. (in press). Electrophysiological indices of intra- and inter-hemispheric visuomotor interaction. In E. Zaidel & M. Iacoboni (Eds.), *The role of the corpus callosum in sensory-motor integration: Anatomy, physiology and behavior.* Cambridge, MA: MIT Press.

Seymour, S., Reuter-Lorenz, P. A., & Gazzaniga, M. S. (1994). The disconnection syndrome: Basic findings reaffirmed. *Brain, 117,* 105–115.

Stelmach, G. E., Amrhein, P. C., & Goggin, N. L. (1988). Age differences in bimanual coordination. *Journal of Gerontology, 43,* 18–23.

Thompson, P., Narr, K., Blanton, R., & Toga, A. (in press). Mapping structural alterations of the corpus callosum during brain development and degeneration. In E. Zaidel & M. Iacoboni (Eds.), *The role of the corpus callosum in sensory-motor integration: Anatomy, physiology and behavior*. Cambridge, MA: MIT Press.

Weis, S., Jellinger, K., & Wegner, E. (1991). Morphometry of the corpus callosum in normal aging and Alzheimer's disease. *Journal of Neural Transmission—Supplementum, 33,* 35–38.

Weller, M. P. I., & Latimer-Sayer, D. T. (1985). Increasing right-hand dominance with age on a motor skill task. *Psychological Medicine, 15,* 867–872.

Witelson, S. F. (1989). Hand and sex differences in the isthmus and genu of the human corpus callosum. A postmortem morphological study. *Brain, 112,* 799–835.

Witelson, S. F. (1991). Sex differences in neuroanatomical changes with aging. *New England Journal of Medicine, 325,* 211–212.

Zaidel, E., & Iacoboni, M. (Eds.). (in press). *The role of the corpus callosum in sensory-motor integration: Anatomy, physiology and behavior.* Cambridge, MA: MIT Press.

Subscription Order Form

Please ❑ enter ❑ renew my subscription to:

DEVELOPMENTAL NEUROPSYCHOLOGY

Volume 17/18, 2000, 6 Issues

8756-5641

Subscription prices per volume:

Individual:	❑ $95.00 US/Canada	❑ $140.00 All Other Countries
Institution:	❑ $645.00 US/Canada	❑ $690.00 All Other Countries
Electronic Only:	❑ $85.50 Individual	❑ $580.50 Institution

Subscriptions are entered on a calendar-year basis only and must be paid in advance in U.S. currency—check, credit card, or money order. Prices for subscriptions include postage and handling. Journal prices expire 12/31/01. NOTE: Institutions must pay institutional rates. Individual subscription orders are welcome if prepaid by credit card or personal check. **Electronic access is available at no additional cost to full-price print subscribers. Electronic-only subscriptions are available at a reduced price.**

❑ Check Enclosed (U.S. Currency Only)

Total Amount Enclosed $________________

❑ Charge My: ❑ VISA ❑ MasterCard ❑ AMEX ❑ Discover

Card Number ______________________________ Exp. Date __________

Signature ____

(Credit card orders cannot be processed without your signature.)

PRINT CLEARLY for proper delivery. STREET ADDRESS/SUITE/ROOM # REQUIRED FOR DELIVERY.

Name ____

Address ____

____

City ______________________ State ______ Zip+4 ____________

Prices are subject to change without notice.

Please note: A $20.00 penalty will be charged against customers providing checks that must be returned for payment. This assessment will be made only in instances when problems in collecting funds are directly attributable to customer error.

For information about online subscriptions, visit our website at *www.erlbaum.com*

LAWRENCE ERLBAUM ASSOCIATES, INC.
JOURNAL SUBSCRIPTION DEPARTMENT
10 INDUSTRIAL AVENUE, MAHWAH, NJ 07430
(201) 236–9500 FAX: (201) 760–3735
TOLL-FREE: 1–800–926–6579